EMERGENCY CAR REPAIRS

Get You Started: Get You Home

Companion Paperfront Titles
Pass Your MOT First Time
What to Watch out for When Buying a Used Car

Car Driving in 2 Weeks
Highway Code Questions and Answers
Learning to Drive in Pictures
Very Advanced Driving
Pass Your Motorcycle L Test

TO **TERESA** and **RACHAEL**

EMERGENCY CAR REPAIRS

GET YOU STARTED: GET YOU HOME

Martin Davies

RIGHT WAY

Printed and bound in Great Britain by Cox & Wyman Ltd., Reading, Berkshire.

The *Right Way* series and the *Paperfronts* series are both published by Elliot Right Way Books, Brighton Road, Lower Kingswood, Tadworth, Surrey, KT20 6TD, U.K.

RESPONSIBILITY

Many of the emergency repairs and methods described in this book are by nature *temporary*. Although author and publisher have taken care to point out pitfalls to the best of their knowledge, it is for the reader to judge whether it is safe to carry out suggestions or drive on in particular circumstances. Neither author nor publisher can accept legal responsibilities for any damage or loss, consequential or otherwise, which may result.

CONTENTS

ILLUSTRATIONS

1
INTRODUCTION

This book is a guide to enable those with no experience or even interest in cars to perform relatively quick emergency repairs at the roadside. The techniques described can often get the car back on the road within minutes and certainly faster than waiting for the professional emergency services. Naturally, this book cannot guarantee to repair the car every time since this depends on what has gone wrong. However, although the book does not cover major problems, it does cover most causes of breakdown, which are so very often trivial and easily fixed. Whilst the majority emphasis concerns restarting a 'dead' engine all other commonly required breakdown procedures are included.

The text is laid out in simple, step-by-step terms with numerous explanatory diagrams, and is based on the assumption that the reader knows 'nothing'. Each chapter deals with a different type of breakdown. Special diagnostic tables augment the text to fast-track you on to the information you need.

Before you drive away . . . or as soon as you get home
The author doesn't insist . . . but you will be better placed when broken down if you have acquainted yourself with the general ideas in this book while the car is still in the garage or driveway. For example, you will learn how expensive overheating can be if allowed to go too far . . . So *do not* wait until you break down. Using the book, find the various engine components using Chapter 4, and practise some of the techniques from later chapters, such as adjusting the fan belt, changing a tyre, etc. Chapter 16 on Working Hints should be especially useful for anyone not mechanically minded. Chapter 17 on routine maintenance outlines the things that really matter.

The following suggestions are jobs you will be pleased to have practised when some real roadside "surgery" comes your way.

1. Find out how to open the bonnet. This might sound silly but the task is only easy "when you know how" (see Chapter 3).
2. Discover where things are in the engine compartment from Chapter 4.
3. Learn how to remove the radiator cap (see Chapter 7, page 94). *Only do this when the engine is cold.*
4. Try adjusting the tension of the fan or drive belt (see Chapter 7C/3, page 101).
5. Learn how to change a fuse, or a light bulb (see Chapter 13).
6. You should be able to change a tyre (see Chapter 15).
7. Unless you have electronic ignition, learn how to adjust the contact breaker points gap (see fig. 7, page 25, and Chapter 5B/3, 1–6) from page 68).

A handy idea, whilst you are having a general look at things, is to find out what the correct tyre pressures are for your car, and what the contact breaker gap (unless you have electronic ignition) and spark plug gaps should be. Look in your owner's instruction handbook, or failing that ask your car dealer. Write these facts on a tacky label and stick it somewhere visible.

This book is limited in scope

My book is designed to get your car going, but it is *not* a car repair manual. It should enable you to complete your journey (in most instances) but then take your car to a garage and get the job assessed, and permanently and properly repaired.

For example, the contact breaker points will often cause trouble and one of the roadside techniques in chapter 5 of this book is simply to rub the opposing surfaces as clean as possible and reset the gap, a two minute job, which may well be sufficient to restart the car. However, the car should be taken to a garage soon, and the points replaced with a new set. The garage can also judge whether the points were simply worn out, or perhaps a faulty capacitor led to their failure and needs replacement as well. As a back-up for readers willing to attempt changing points themselves, the full details are given later in the same chapter.

Further, this book is intended to be universal, being applicable to any make and model of petrol-engined car. Because of this the location of the various engine components will vary, as will some of the techniques described. However, the text has been designed largely to overcome any differences so that the various components can be identified and the different techniques performed regardless of the make of the car, although diesel engines are not covered. If you do come across a variation that has you puzzled, a common-sense approach should see you through.

Finally, do not be afraid of your car and the "unknown" it represents. Car repairs and especially those described here are indeed easy "when you know how" and there is certainly no "magic" attached to them.

How to use this book:
The main elements of the book are Chapters 5, and 7 to 15, each of which deals with a different kind of breakdown. Each of these is subdivided into sections dealing with the different major causes of the breakdown (e.g. 5A, 5B . . . etc). Each section is then further divided (e.g. 5A/1, 5A/2 . . . etc) wherever this will be helpful for faster cross-reference. The other chapters at the beginning and end of the book do not deal with breakdowns but consist of useful information about safety, routine maintenance etc. Chapter 6 is on emergency Jump-Lead and Bump starting.

Safety **do's** *and* **don'ts**
Read the following before attempting any of the jobs outlined in this book.

1. **Do** use common-sense – think before acting.
2. **Don't** let familiarity breed contempt – **do** always treat your car as potentially dangerous and lethal.
3. **Don't** start the engine without making sure that the gear lever is in neutral and the handbrake is on.
4. Some procedures are carried out with the engine going – **do** be very careful of the moving parts especially the fan and fan belt where, because of the speed, it is not always

apparent that it is moving. *Clothing:* **don't** wear loose clothing e.g., cuffs, ties and scarves, which could be caught up if engine is running. **Do** remove watches and rings.

5. **Do** be careful of electric fans which can start up even with the engine switched off (see Chapter 7C/1).
6. Electrical circuits: **do** make sure that the ignition is turned off before touching anything – better still although slightly inconvenient, do remove the key from the ignition and put it in your pocket. **Don't** touch live wires with bare hands, e.g. when testing for a spark (Chapter 5B/2) – use an insulated pair of pliers. **Do** keep spark tests away from the carburettor or fuel lines. **Don't** smoke during *any* investigations.
7. Cooling system: **don't** release radiator cap until engine properly cooled (Chapter 7).
8. Engine block: all parts of the engine block are very hot after engine running – **don't** touch it with bare hands; **do** bring your hand up to it slowly and you will feel heat given off from it. In a cramped engine compartment it is possible to touch one hot component by mistake, withdraw the hand rapidly (natural reaction) only to touch a second hot component.
9. Oil: **don't** touch leaking oil as it is very hot and tends to stick to the skin.
10. Jacking-up the car: **don't** put your explicit trust in the jack; **don't** get underneath a car that is only held up by a jack; **do** try and keep as far away from the car as possible when working on it, in case it slips off the jack. When undoing fully-tightened wheel-nuts **do** slacken them off while the wheels are still on the ground – the same applies to retightening the wheel-nuts. When taking off the actual wheel **do** it gently, **don't** jerk it off.
11. Weight: **don't** attempt any lifting that might cause a problem. **Do** expect everything to be heavy e.g. wheels, bonnet.
12. Undoing nuts and bolts: **do** use the proper-sized spanner.
13. Time: **do** take your time. **Don't** rush.
14. **Do** consider safety of passengers in a roadside emergency, especially on motorways where many unnecessary accidents happen.

2

TOOLS, EQUIPMENT AND SPARES

Here are listed tools, equipment and spares that should be permanently carried in the car. Essential items in each checklist come first. The remainder are desirable. Don't invest in cheap spanners or screwdrivers – when encountering a stiff nut or screw for the first time, they tend to bend or slip, burring over the item, which can then be almost impossible to release.

Tools checklist

Essential tools

Screwdriver set (assorted screwdrivers including Phillips-types).

Spanner set, open-ended. Spanner sizes are measured in either metric or non-metric units. Any dealer in your make can advise exactly which types will fit your car. Generally a metric set will fit more nuts on most cars. A medium size adjustable spanner is useful too.

Spark plug spanner. (Check if your engine requires a special design.)

Adjustable self-grip wrench.

A pair of pliers with insulated handles.

Jack, and wheel-nut spanner (normally supplied with car).

Desirable tools and equipment

Hammer – cheap versions of this tool are usually O.K.

Fluid for sealing leaks in the radiator (from motorists' D.I.Y. stores).

Extension bar. Handy since it is used to apply that much more pressure to release tight wheel-nuts (see fig. 56, page 146).

Pen-knife.

Pair of tweezers.

Feeler gauge set, for measuring contact breaker points gap, sparking plug gaps. Spark plug gap-adjusting tool.

Foot pump with pressure gauge – or separate tyre pressure gauge.

Water hose repair kit (from motorists' D.I.Y. stores), or spare hoses.

Old toothbrushes.

String.

Insulating tape, in narrow and wide sizes.

Selection of jubilee clips to match radiator hoses etc.

Old rags/clothes.

Small magnet.

Torch.

Spray-can of penetrating oil such as WD40.

Groundsheet for lying on.

Aerosol spray for removing condensation from the ignition system during damp weather (from motorists' D.I.Y. stores). Better still is to use an *inhibitor* spray before the onset of damp weather. This can "seal" the electrics quite effectively.

A stick of white chalk (see Chapter 5B/4 for use).

Battery jump leads for starting car when battery is flat. N.B. – indispensable if you have automatic transmission. *Buy thickest leads available. Beware of cheap brands, too thin to carry the necessary electric current.*

Aluminium baking-foil (small sheet).

Emery paper – medium grade.

Jelly for cleaning hands, such as Swarfega (from motorists' D.I.Y. stores).

3 metres household lighting flex, or Low Tension grade car ignition electrical wire.

Household rubber gloves, to insulate from electric shocks and/or to avoid dirty hands.

Spares Checklist

Vital spares to carry

Car maker's owner's operating instruction handbook.*

Spare wheel and tyre, fully inflated.*

Fan belt/drive belt(s) – either the correct belt(s) for your particular car or one of the universal emergency belts which will fit any type of car and can be fitted without undoing any nuts and bolts – available from motorists' D.I.Y. stores or your car dealer (see Chapter 7C/2).

Petrol – carried only in a container sold for this purpose.

Spare fuses (there may be more than one type; it's best to have 2–3 of each handy).

Fire extinguisher.

FIRST AID kit. (The excellent boxed kits on sale are handily kept in the car. Make sure cream etc., for dealing with burns is included. It's all too easy to touch a hot engine or exhaust pipe without thinking . . .)

Very useful spares to have with you

Make sure that the specialised spares, e.g. contact breaker points, capacitor, etc. are of the correct type for your particular car.

*As supplied with car.

A set of contact breaker points.†

Capacitor (also known as a condenser).†

Light bulbs: main bulbs (– unless sealed units are fitted as they are quite expensive), sidelight bulbs, indicator bulbs, brake lights.

Engine oil (5 litre can).

Water (ready-mixed with anti-freeze for preference) best carried in a large polythene jerrycan.

Spare radiator cap, if a spring-loaded type is fitted (see Chapter 4, page 29, and Chapter 7D).

Spare spark plugs. (Must be of exact grade and type specified by makers; substitutes will not do.) A new set is the best thing to have; otherwise a selection of old ones – known to be working – kept by, can be very handy.

Emergency windscreen – from motorists' D.I.Y. stores etc.

†Note – these are not needed if your car has electronic ignition.

Old components

It is well worth saving certain old components, particularly spark plugs, contact breaker points, capacitor and other ignition items – from the times you replace them for efficient engine running, even though they still work O.K. They can come into their own in an emergency.

3

HOW TO OPEN THE BONNET

1. Most bonnets are unlatched from the inside of the car by a lever located in the front at leg level, usually on the driver's side. (Some cars have the lever elsewhere, consult your owner's instruction handbook.) When pulled, this lever opens the bonnet slightly; generally it then remains held on a second catch.
2. The second catch is located under the front edge of the bonnet (on the end away from the hinges) and is a hooked piece of metal which is moved up, down or sideways, so releasing the bonnet. Although this catch can be located by searching with the fingers under the edge of the bonnet, it is best found by bending down and looking under the bonnet edge. The bonnet may rise either from the front or the rear end of the engine compartment; in the latter type the second catch is usually absent.
3. Now raise the bonnet, *but* be prepared for something that can be quite heavy.
4. The raised bonnet may be fixed in position by means of a metal prop which is attached to the bodywork and lies parallel to it just in front of the radiator. When swung into position the prop locates in a hole in the underside of the bonnet. Alternatively, the prop might be hinged to the underside of the bonnet so that when pulled out it can locate in a hole on the inside of the car's wing. Or, there may be a permanent hinged or spring-loaded device which may need to be "locked" in position (as described in the owner's instruction handbook – although normally obvious), or automatic telescopic stays. *Important*: make sure that the bonnet is secure before letting go of it or sticking your head under it!

4

ENGINE COMPARTMENT LAYOUT

The positions of individual components vary from car to car and from model to model. However, the components which you need to identify are easily found, either because of their distinctive shape, or because of their relationship with other identifiable components. Whatever make of car you own, a distributor looks like a distributor, a carburettor like a carburettor, etc. Despite the best efforts of modern engineers to design better and more complex engines, the shape of the basic different engine components appears immutable.

The engine
First open the bonnet and secure it in position (see previous chapter) to reveal the engine compartment; compare the general layout with figs. 1(a) and 1(b). The ENGINE will face one of the ways shown. Compare the engine with fig. 2 (viewed (a) from the fan/drive belt end of the engine, and (b) from on top). Figs. 2(a) and (b) are stylised *general* diagrams – the specifics of your own engine will almost certainly differ.

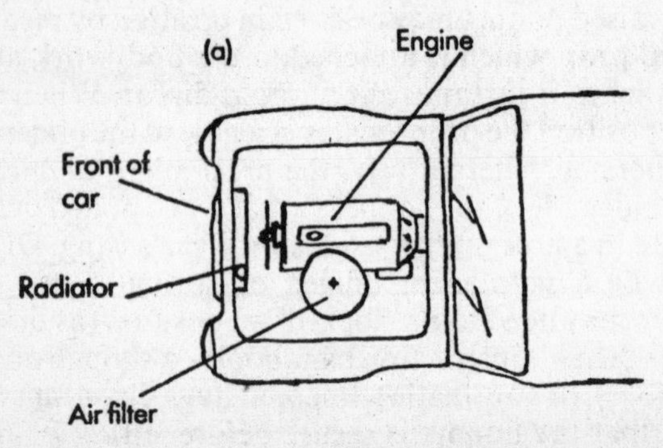

Fig. 1: (a) Longitudinal Engine

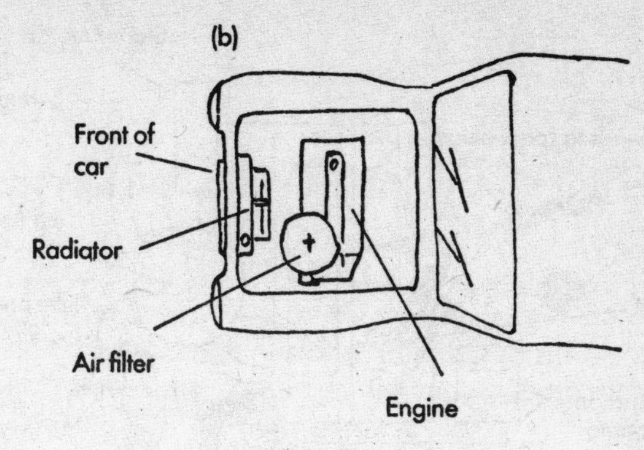

Fig. 1: (b) Transverse Engine

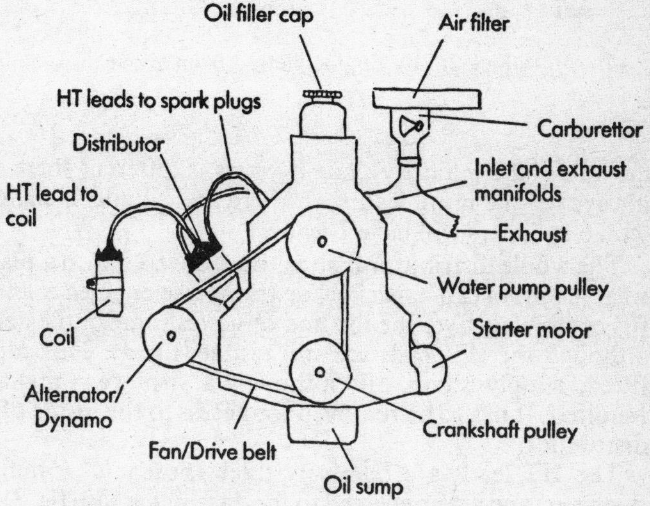

Fig. 2: (a) Engine viewed from the front

The ignition system
Next, locate the DISTRIBUTOR (fig. 3) which looks like a multi-armed octopus – it is cylindrical, about the size of a large fist, with a usually black or brown plastic top half, that has five HIGH TENSION (HT) LEADS (or CABLES) coming out of it. This number of leads applies to cars which have four

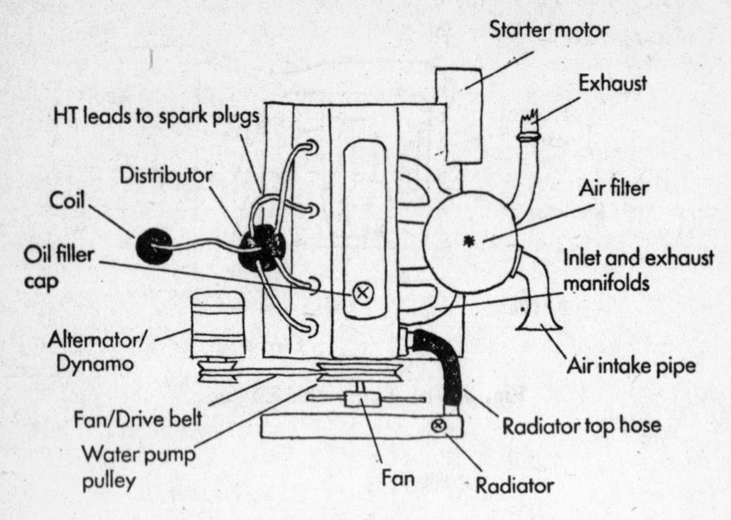

Fig. 2: (b) Engine viewed from above

cylinders (the majority), but if yours is different there will always be one more lead than there are cylinders, e.g. cars with 6 cylinders will have 7 leads.

The whole distributor is sometimes covered with a plastic weather-proof cap, especially on transverse-engined cars; this fits completely over the top and obscures some of the detail, although the HT leads are still visible (fig. 4). This cap, if fitted, simply slides off, although a firm tug might be required. It has to be removed for access to the inside of the distributor.

The HT leads are relatively thick (nearly ¼″ (5mm) in diameter) and are connected to the distributor cap (fig. 3) in a standard arrangement whereby there is one lead in the centre of the cap, with the remainder of the leads arranged around the edge. The centre lead goes to the COIL (fig. 5), which is mounted on the engine or bodywork. The leads around the edge go towards the engine and connect with the SPARK PLUGS, which are screwed directly into the engine cylinder block itself. The HT leads carry the high voltage – big spark – current, serving the plugs. The thin wire between the coil and the distributor is part of the LOW TENSION (LT) CIRCUIT, as is the other thin wire leading from the coil which connects to the battery via the ignition switch. The LT circuit feeds the HT circuit. Low tension current is multiplied at the coil, into the high tension big spark current.

You can remove the cap of the distributor by undoing the two clips which hold it in place (see Chapter 5B/3, page 68). Underneath (unless you have electronic ignition for which see further below) are the CONTACT BREAKER POINTS (also simply known as "the points") and the ROTOR ARM, which

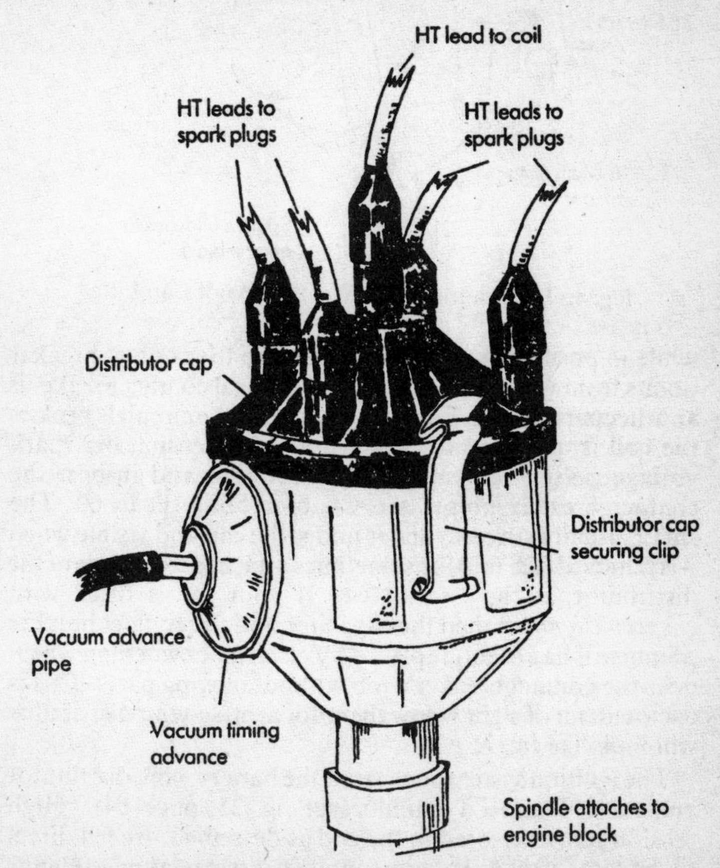

Fig. 3: External View of a Distributor

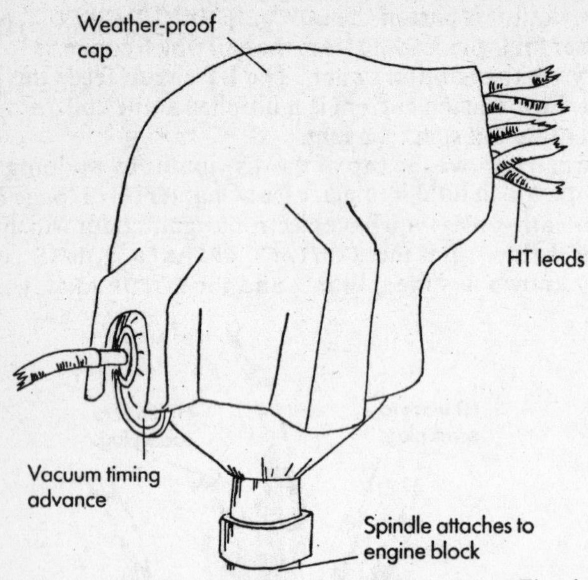

Fig. 4: Distributor with a Weather-Proof Cap Fitted

while in position, will partially obscure the contact breaker points from view (fig. 6(a)). The mechnical contact breaker is another part of the LT circuit. Each time the circuit is broken the coil is activated to produce its high tension big spark voltage pulse. To remove the rotor arm and inspect the contact breaker points see Chapter 5B/3, page 69. The small, usually silver, cylinder under the cap and visible when it is removed (fig. 6(b)) or sometimes attached to the side of the distributor, is the CAPACITOR. If your car is fitted with *electronic ignition* then the capacitor and the contact breaker points will be absent, replaced by electronic switching which does the contact breaker's job without moving parts. This is enclosed out of sight below the rotor arm, so your distributor will look like fig. 7.

The ignition system consists of the battery, coil, distributor and the HT and LT circuits (see fig. 25, page 64). High tension sparks created in the coil as described, are fed direct to the rotor arm. As it whirs round, in direct relation to engine speed, the sparks are distributed out down each spark plug

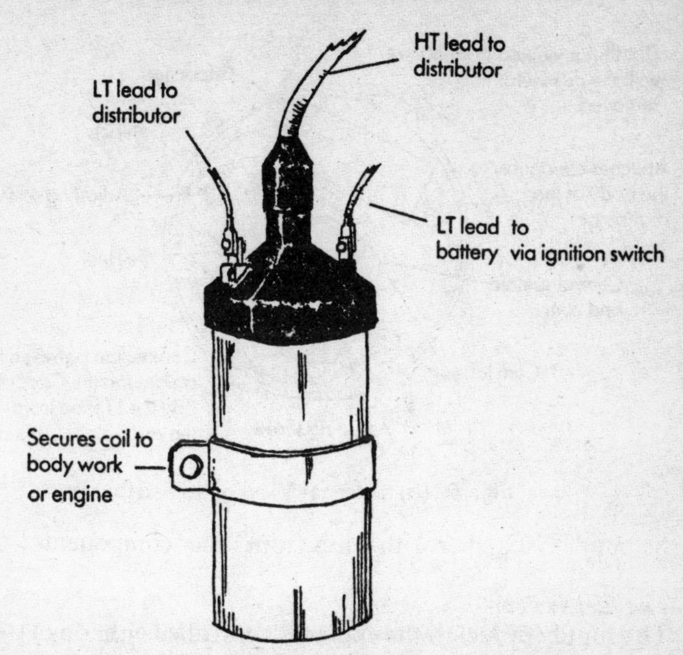

Fig. 5: Coil

lead in the correct order and timed so each plug fires at just the right moment. It must be stressed that the electrical system in general is often difficult to trace. For example, the thin wires between the coil and the battery (via the ignition switch) will probably be difficult to follow in their entirety because the wires, within a short distance from the coil, will

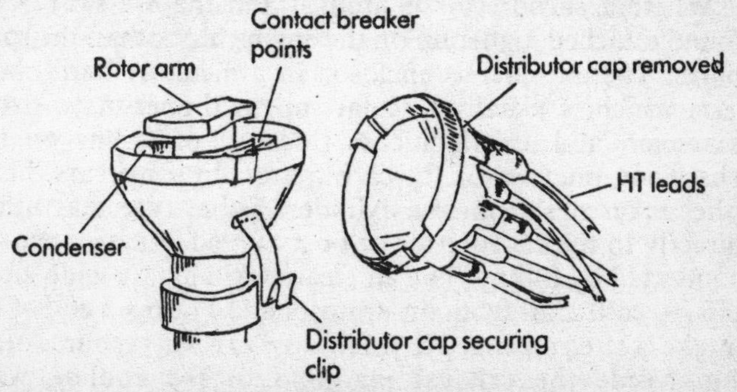

Fig. 6: (a) Distributor cap removed

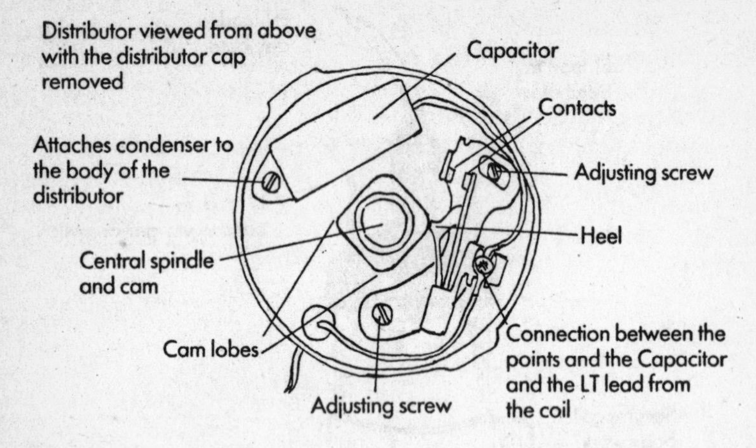

Fig. 6: (b) Internal View of a Distributor

be bundled together with wires from other components.

The fuel system

The supply of fuel to the engine is controlled either by FUEL INJECTION or by a CARBURETTOR.

On a fuel injected engine a spider's web of braided metal pipes fanning out from one source, has a pipe screwed into the engine block for each cylinder – the same number as there are sparking plugs. The other side of that source will be found the AIR FILTER case, the whole arrangement normally mounted to one side of the engine. See lower part of fig. 8.

Where a carburettor is used, it and the AIR FILTER are found attached higher up on the engine block than the spark plugs. The air filter is enclosed in a metal or hard-plastic case which is usually circular, up to dinner-plate size in diameter, and several inches thick. It often sits on top, obscuring the view of the carburettor. In some cars the air filter takes the form of a cylinder. Either type may attach directly to the carburettor or be mounted at a distance and connected by tubing. The air cleaner will have a wide intake pipe to collect air from the atmosphere. The open end of this intake is often arranged to reach close to a warm source of air, e.g. beside the exhaust manifold or the cooling water radiator. See upper half of fig. 8.

The carburettor is identified as probably the most complicated component with cables and tubes attached to it. If still in doubt about where yours is, follow the exhaust pipe where it enters the engine compartment and joins the engine block, if necessary by tracing it from the rear of the car. The exhaust pipe is connected to the engine block via the exhaust manifold. This is a metal structure which fans out in the form of "fingers", one for each cylinder, and which are joined to

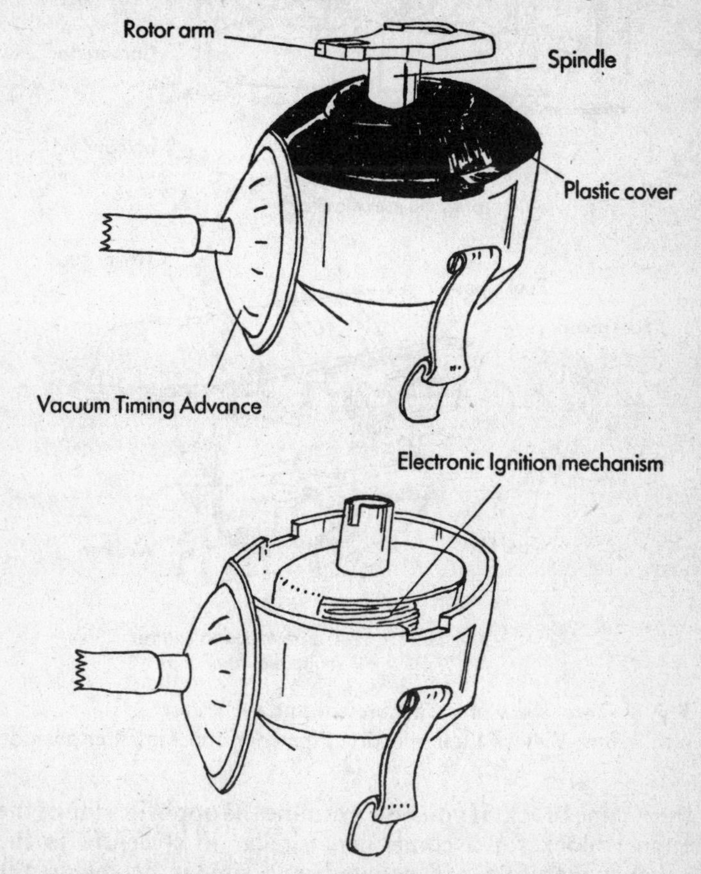

Fig. 7: Recognition picture for Electronic Ignition
Top: With Distributor Cap Removed
Below: With Distributor Cap, Rotor Arm and Plastic Cover Removed

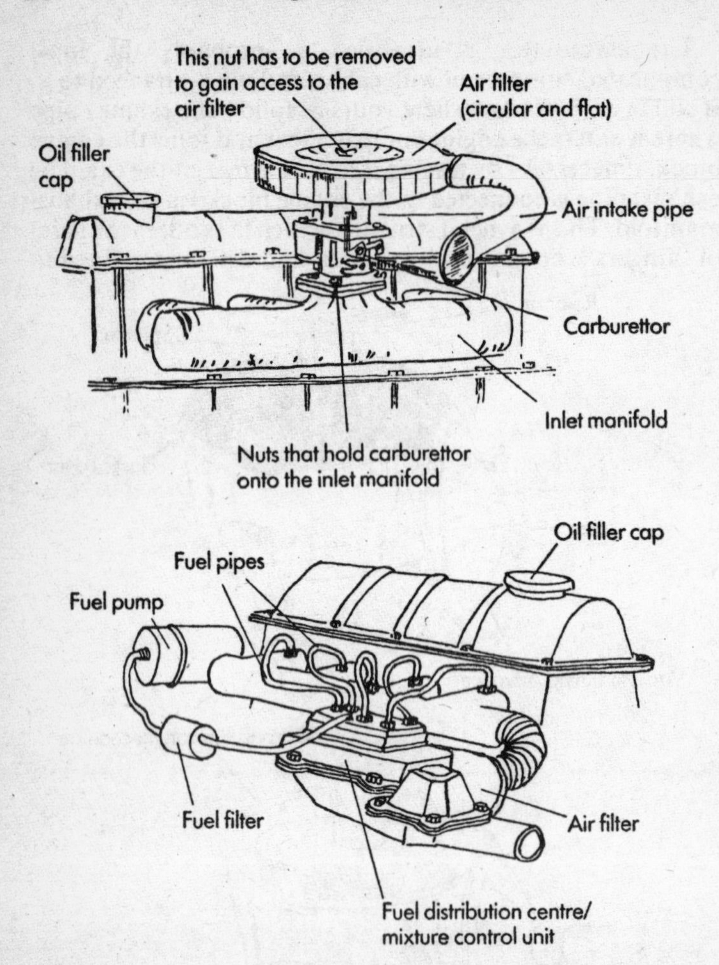

Fig. 8: *Top:* View of a Carburettor and Air Filter and, *below:* View of Fuel Injection Pipework and Air Filter position

the engine block. If you now examine the opposite side of the engine block for a component similar in structure to the exhaust manifold and situated at a similar height up the engine block, you should find the inlet manifold onto which is bolted the carburettor. The example just described, and shown by fig. 9, is of a cross-flow engine. Other engines may have their exhaust and inlet manifolds attached to the same side of the engine block, or have both structures sitting atop a wider, flatter engine block. Whatever design is used the carburettor will be bolted to the inlet manifold.

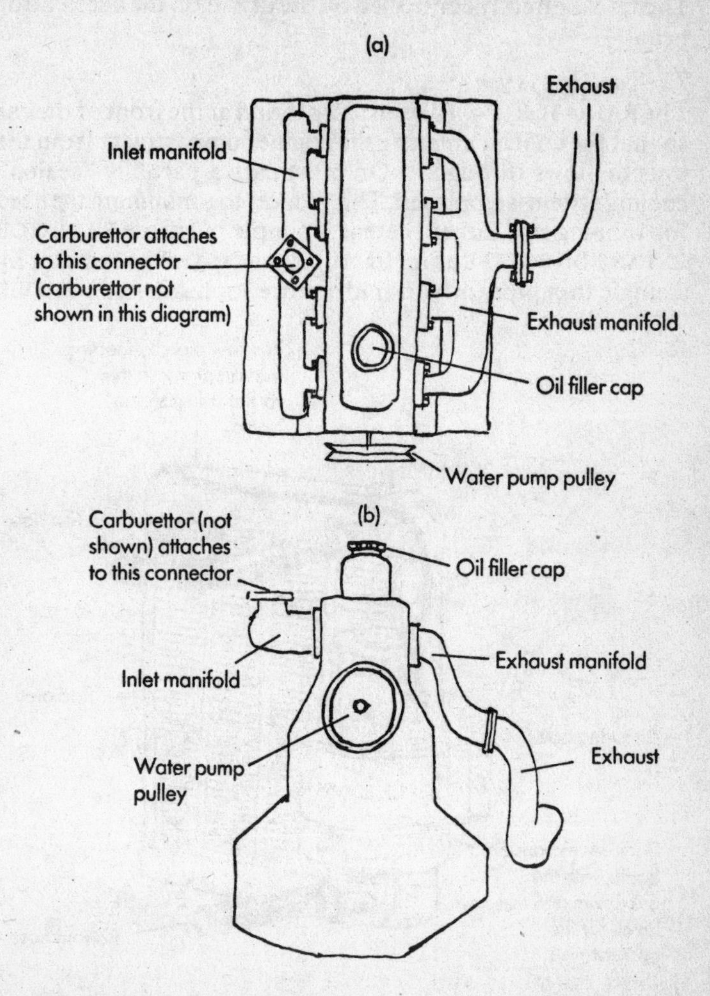

Fig. 9: Example Location of the Inlet and Exhaust Manifolds
(a) Engine Viewed from Above
(b) Engine Viewed from the Front

The job of the carburettor or fuel injection system is to mix petrol and air into just the right combustible mixture and deliver this for burning in the engine cylinders at the precise rate required for optimal efficiency at any given engine speed. The rate is directly controlled by the driver on the accelerator pedal.

The cooling system

The RADIATOR (fig. 10) is usually found at the front of the car so that the cool air entering the engine compartment from the outside flows through it. On most cars a partially "sealed" cooling system is employed. This reduces to a minimum the need for topping up. Either there is a simple overflow RADIATOR EXPANSION BOTTLE as in (fig. 10) connected to the radiator by a single thin pipe, or you find a more sophisticated HEADER

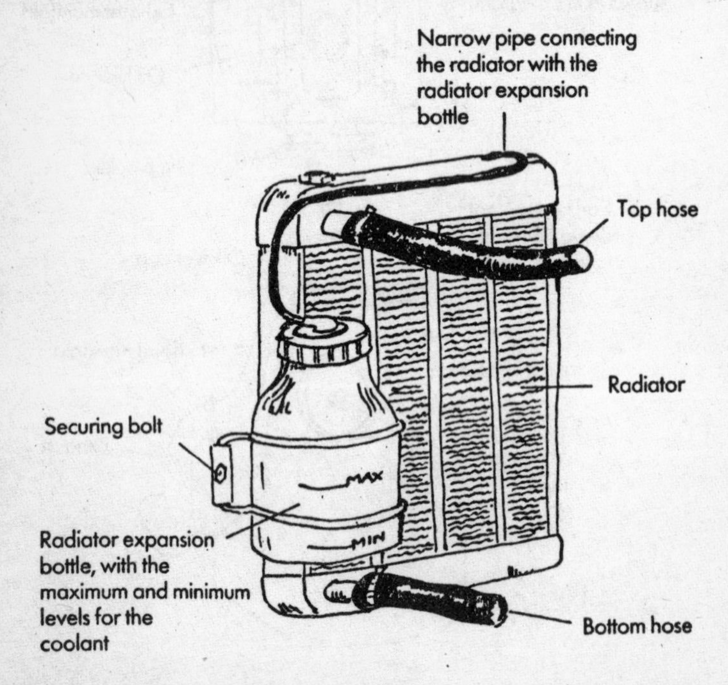

Fig. 10: Radiator Expansion Bottle
For clarity, the fan and engine block have been omitted from this figure. Beware! Do not touch when hot.

EXPANSION TANK with both inflow and outflow piping. On older cars no such expansion system is used. Coolant (water with anti-freeze; see Chapter 7) on such older cars is added directly via the RADIATOR CAP. Where the simple expansion bottle is used, *coolant is always topped up via the bottle*; however a radiator cap is normally also provided so you can make sure the radiator itself is also full – as it must be kept. Where a header tank is fitted there is usually no radiator cap and coolant can only be added via the header tank.

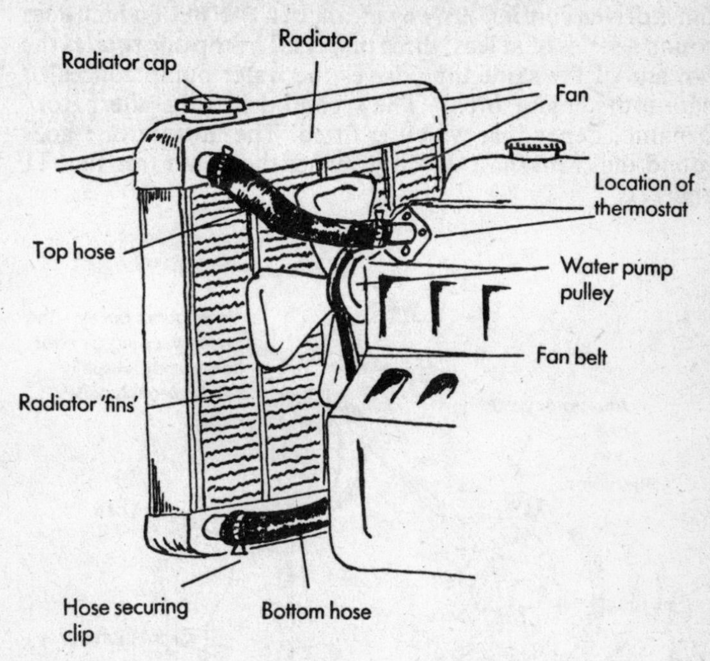

Fig. 11: Radiator, plus Thermostat and Water Pump Locations. Beware! Do not touch when hot. This design has a fan which is driven continuously by the crankshaft pulley, via a fan belt which also drives the dynamo pulley.

There are two thick hoses attached to the radiator, one at the top and the other at the bottom. They are up to twice as thick as garden hose, made in black rubber. The top hose goes towards the engine block and inside the bulbous housing where it joins the engine block (fig. 11) is the THERMOSTAT. In a small minority of cars, the thermostat is located by following the bottom hose (see also Chapter 7E, page 103 and figs. 43/44).

Some cars are air-cooled, in which case there is no radiator.

The pulley system and the charging system

Cool air is drawn across the radiator by the action of a FAN which is located directly behind the radiator. In some cars this fan is driven continuously by means of a FAN BELT which goes round a series of at least three pulleys. The top one rotates the fan and at the same time drives the water pump concealed within the engine block. The second drives the alternator/dynamo, depending which is fitted. The bottom one goes round the crankshaft which provides the power (see figs. 11 and 12).

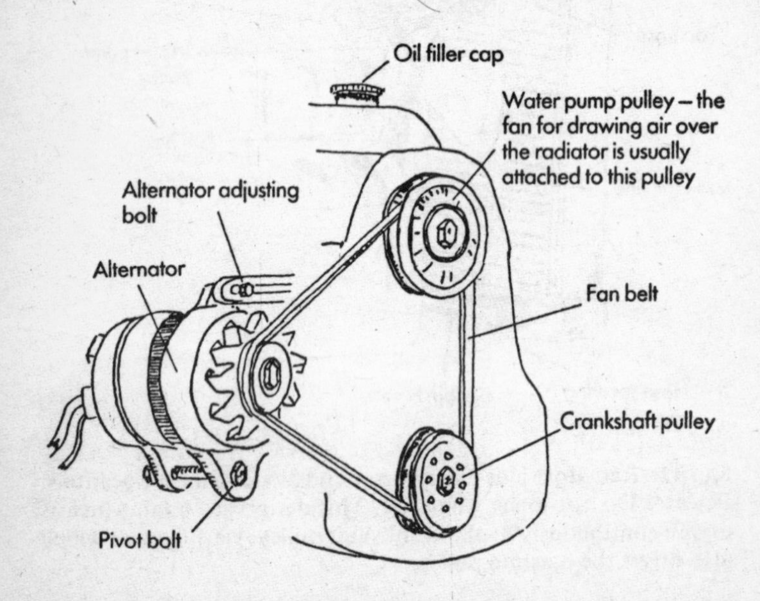

Fig. 12: Pulley Drive-Belt System
This engine is fitted with an alternator. A car fitted with a dynamo would appear the same except that the alternator would be replaced by a dynamo, also tube shaped but having a longer body.

On other cars an electric fan is employed (see Chapter 7C, page 97) which is operated by an electric motor and does not require a fan belt (fig. 13). However, even on those cars with an electric fan, there is still a DRIVE BELT which drives the water pump and the alternator/dynamo. Regardless of the type of fan, the drive belt still goes round three basic pulleys (alternator/dynamo, water pump and crankshaft) and although there are variations using two or more belts, the arrangement of the pulleys is always essentially the same.

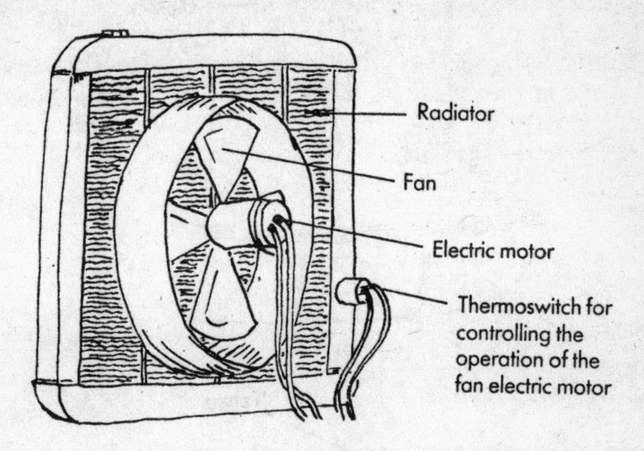

Fig. 13: Electric Fan. Beware! These fans can start up without warning, even when the ignition is switched off.

The ALTERNATOR or DYNAMO provides electricity to run the engine and to keep the battery (which is needed to start the engine) charged. It is cylindrical in shape (alternators are short and wide while dynamos are thinner and longer). As is evident from fig. 12 the alternator/dynamo is located to one side of the engine. Its position is fully adjustable and it has wires coming out of the back of it. Moving the position of the alternator/dynamo provides the means by which the drive belt can be tightened or slackened during fitting or adjustment.

The lubrication system

The moving components of your engine have to be well

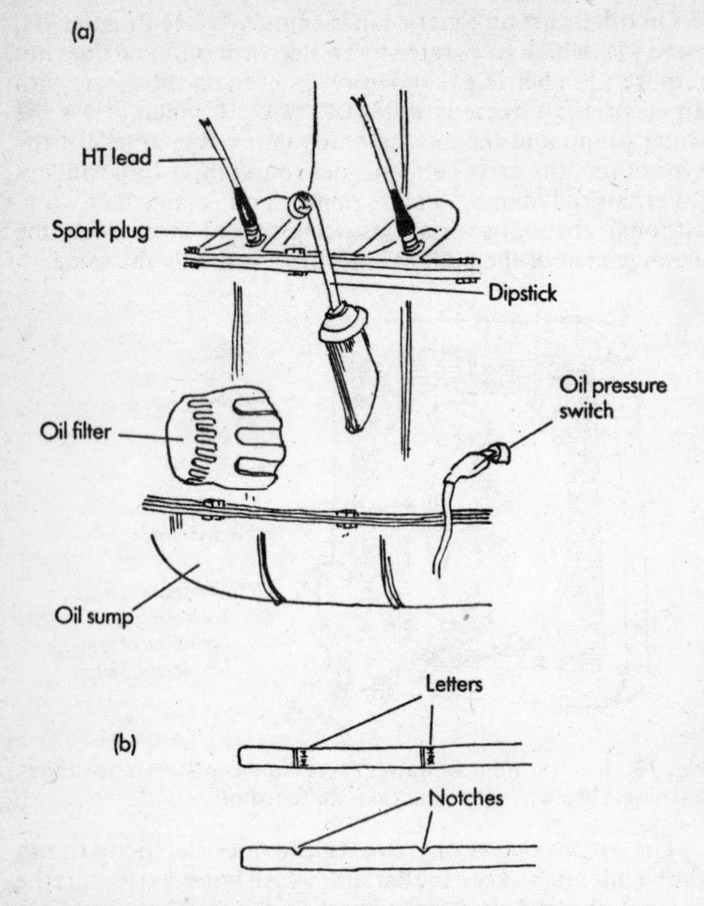

Fig 14: Dipstick. Oil Filter and Oil Pressure Switch
(a) View of the Different Components
(b) Examples of the Measuring Marks on a Dipstick
The letters or the notches or other indicators show the maximum and minimum levels of the oil in the car's engine. The difference between MAX and MIN is usually about one litre; test or check the owner's instruction handbook to find out. Do not overfill.
With car on level ground. withdraw the dipstick and wipe it clean. Allow a minute after the engine is stopped for most oil to drain down to sump. Insert dipstick fully – then withdraw to get a true reading. Remember to replace dipstick.

lubricated, a job performed by oil, circulating under pressure. Small amounts of oil are used up, over time. There are therefore means for adding oil to the engine (oil filler cap), for measuring its level (dipstick), for keeping the oil clean (oil filter), and for telling the driver when the oil pressure drops too low (oil pressure switch, and warning lamp or gauge).

The OIL FILLER CAP is located on the very top of the engine. The dipstick and oil filter positions vary considerably; an indication of their location should be obtained by consulting your owner's instruction handbook. The DIPSTICK is usually located on the side of the engine, usually about halfway down. Quite often only the small grabhandle part can be seen initially, and this appears to sit atop a narrow metal tube rising from one side of the engine to a convenient position (fig. 14).

The OIL FILTER, often near the dipstick (although do not necessarily expect yours to be) is located further down on the engine block, almost at the very bottom. It is cylindrical, about the size of a giant coffee mug, and for convenience of replacement at service intervals, is screwed directly into the engine block. The oil filter usually provides a touch of colour, blue, orange or yellow being favourites, and may have the words "oil filter" printed on it. On older cars a similar shaped housing, probably of engine colour, conceals an oil filter, these are more tricky to renew because the housing itself, not being a throw-away item, has always carefully to be re-fitted. Situated quite close to the oil filter and the dipstick is the likely place for an electrical connection directly into the engine block which is the OIL PRESSURE SWITCH (fig. 14).

The battery

The BATTERY (fig. 15) is usually located in one of the top corners of the engine compartment, but can be anywhere e.g. behind a side panel of the boot. It is a rectangular box of approximately gentlemen's shoe-box size. There is an electrical terminal on top at each end, one marked positive (+) and/or colour-coded red, and the other negative (–) and/or coded black; each has a thick cable attached. The lead attached to the negative terminal is usually the earth lead; it is

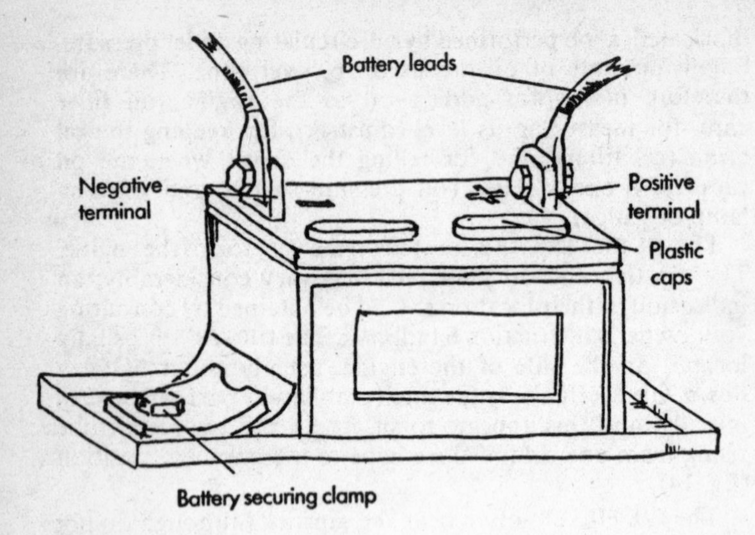

Fig. 15: Battery
On a few expensive batteries, electrolyte can only be topped up by a service agent.

quite short and attached to the bodywork of the car or the engine block. Sometimes thick braided wire is used for this instead of insulated cable. The insulated cable attached to the positive (output) terminal supplies the electricity to the ignition system for starting the car and to operate the electrical systems in the car when the engine is not running. In car electrical circuits there is no need to have an earth return wire for every component. Circuits are completed via the metal body of the car itself. Thus positive current is wired to an instrument panel light or whatever: it comes back to earth through the body. There are a few old cars where the earth return is to positive and current is sourced from the negative side, i.e. the opposite way round, but these are now rare.

The fuse-box
This may be in the engine compartment attached to one of the side walls, or sometimes it is in the passenger compartment behind the dashboard. Its exact location and the electrical components that the different fuses serve can be found in your owner's instruction handbook. The fuse-box lid may be

opaque, or transparent – which helps you find it because you can see the fuses; a code to denote which fuses protect which circuits is often printed inside it. For suspect fuses see chapter 12A and fig. 52.

The starter motor

The STARTER MOTOR is an electric motor which turns the engine in order to make it start. It is probably the hardest of our components to locate. It is usually placed low down on the engine block towards the rear on longitudinally mounted engines and often on the right-hand side as you look at the engine from the front of the car, i.e. it is at one of the bottom back corners of the engine cylinder block. In cars with transversely mounted engines, the starter motor frequently occupies the same relative position, remembering of course that the engine has been turned anti-clockwise through 90° (figs. 1 and 2). The starter motor is cylindrical in shape, of a similar size to the dynamo or alternator but with no pulley attached to it. If the car has what is called a pre-engaged starter motor then there will be a smaller cylinder which is the SOLENOID mounted directly on top of it. In cars with an inertia-type starter (usually older models), the solenoid is separate and can be found by tracing the wires from the back of the starter motor a short distance to a "cross-like" structure (the solenoid) which is bolted to the bodywork. The solenoid might be the one component that you should seek help on to locate, although once you know what you are looking for you will be able to find it on any make of car (see fig. 16(b) and (c)).

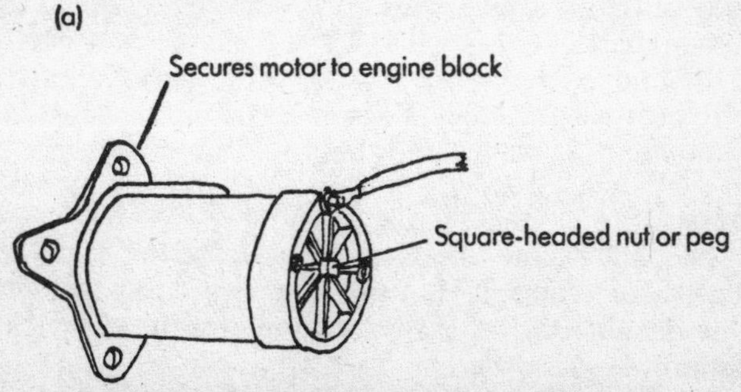

Fig. 16: (a) Inertia-type Starter Motor

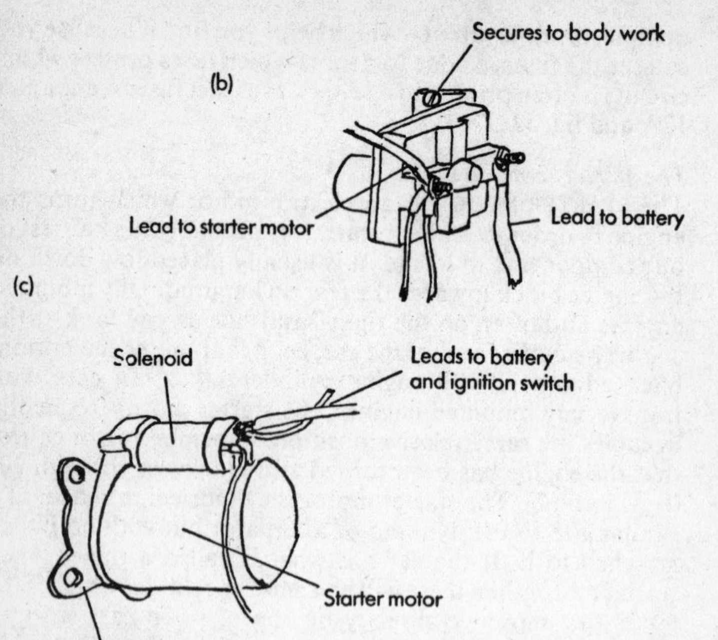

Fig. 16: (b) Solenoid
(c) Pre-engaged Starter Motor.

5

ENGINE WON'T GO

Chapter 4 helped you find your way around under the bonnet. You may need to refer back to it in order to understand the present chapter properly. But first . . .

Roadside safety

- ⋆ Hazard warning lights ON if appropriate.
- ⋆ Get the car off the road if possible.
- ⋆ Handbrake on and gear lever in neutral (or selector in P, Park).
- ⋆ Switch off ignition (especially in event of fire) *and remove key*.
- ⋆ Fire! Get passengers out at once, well away from danger of explosion; also see below.

BUT . . .

- ⋆ Take care getting out of the car. Use nearside doors if possible on fast roads.
- ⋆ Don't wander round car absentmindedly or let people stand around behind it (they may obscure the hazard flashers).
- ⋆ Set out warning triangle (if you have it), 50 metres back up the road.
- ⋆ Keep passengers and pets under control.
- ⋆ Don't smoke – petrol may be leaking.

IN THE CASE OF FIRE . . .

1. Lose no time calling the Fire Brigade to any serious fire. Warn passengers/bystanders to stay well clear.
2. *Provided there is no petrol spillage, or danger thereof*:

   a) A small fire such as smouldering upholstery or wiring can be attacked with a fire extinguisher or, if you can do it before flames take a significant hold, it can sometimes be smothered with a blanket etc.

b) Do not open the bonnet unless you believe you will be able to tackle fire under it yourself. A fire there may be too powerful to risk opening it yourself; however, do pull the bonnet release catch if it is inside the car, if possible. (This will enable the Fire Brigade professionals to get the bonnet open.)

c) Subject to being able to get at it safely, once the fire is under control disconnect the battery, see page 49, to prevent further short circuits etc. etc.

d) Make sure any fire you have managed to control, is put completely out so it cannot flare again.

The above warnings apply with redoubled force on motorways, where the warning triangle should be set out 150 metres back on the hard shoulder, not the carriageway.

Now, what is the problem?

Apart from major breakdowns beyond our scope, the problem *when the engine won't go* is almost always one of 3 things:-

BATTERY trouble .... **SECTION 5A**
No spark to ignite fuel (SPARK ELECTRICS), or **SECTION 5B**
FUEL SUPPLY .... **SECTION 5C**

We now probe these 3 areas (noting how they interlink), starting from any clues we might glean from how the engine conked out.

BEWARE! Your battery only contains a finite amount of electric power. Once it starts to flag your chances of starting the engine easily are much reduced! THINK before you punish the battery trying in vain. Even a push may not help once you wreck it! See under BATTERY (section 5A/4, page 46, and for push starts, tow starts and using battery jump leads with another car, see chapter 6).

Start with the *clues* below. Your suspicions may then take you direct to one of the 3 major areas just mentioned, in which case go straight to that heading. If not, work through this chapter systematically – it has been designed to pinpoint the most likely faults first. Table 1, the master plan which follows these clues, should direct you to the next section you need.

Clues for short cuts

How did your engine run before it stopped?

Observation	*What to suspect first*
Sudden dramatic loss of power.	1) Engine seizure – overheating due to lack of water or oil (chapter 7). 2) Break in ignition low tension circuit, SPARK ELECTRICS (section 5B/3, page 63).
Progressive spluttering for ½ a mile or less.	Run out of petrol, FUEL SUPPLY (sections 5B/1 page 58 and 5C/1, page 85).
Misfiring, worsening over several miles; regular mis-beat can be heard, pulling power much reduced, gear lever may even shake under normal load, some overheating may be evident.	SPARK ELECTRICS (section 5B from page 58 – especially contact breaker points, page 66, and Chapter 9, engine misfires, page 120). If Battery also now flat, suspect charging system, page 117.
With increasing difficulty in starting (despite good battery) for some days or weeks – warm up taking ever longer.	SPARK ELECTRICS (sections 5B/2–5B/5 from page 59).
"Lumpy" – rhythmical fast/slow tick-over, tending to stall, puff-puff rather than regular exhaust note.	Choke left out by mistake. Choked air cleaner. FUEL SUPPLY (sections 5C/1 and 5C/2 from page 85).
Perfectly O.K. yesterday!	1) Dampness/condensation affecting electrical leads SPARK ELECTRICS (section 5B/2, page 59). 2) Flooding – possibly too much choke (section 5A/4, page 47).

What is happening when you try to start the engine?

Observation	*What to suspect first*
Silence.	1) BATTERY – flat, or having loose connections (section 5A/6, page 49). 2) Poor connections to starter solenoid and/or starter. (Section 5A/7, page 51.) 3) Fault in starter motor (section 5A/7, page 51).
Starter whirs strangely but doesn't turn engine, or single muted click is the only response.	Ditto: 1), 2) or 3).
Starter vigorous to begin with but flagging after repeated attempts.	Your technique! Have you flooded the engine or left the choke out? (Section 5A/4, page 46.) And BATTERY (sections 5A/1–5A/5 from page 42).
Starter sounds dead-beat from first attempt.	1) Battery low – were lights or ignition left on? (Section 5A/5 page 48.) Has a loose drive-belt prevented proper re-charging? (Chapter 7C/3 page 101.) BATTERY (loose connections, section 5A/6, page 49). 2) Starter motor faulty (section 5A/7 page 51).
Starter very willing but no signs of engine firing into life.	SPARK ELECTRICS (sections 5B/1–5B/5 from page 58) – especially on damp mornings with heavy condensation. Battery connections loose or corroded.
Starter working hard, engine tries – definitely kicks itself over once or twice – but won't go.	1) Empty petrol tank or leakage, flooding, clogged-up air cleaner, FUEL SUPPLY (sections 5B/1 and 5C/1 and 5C/2).

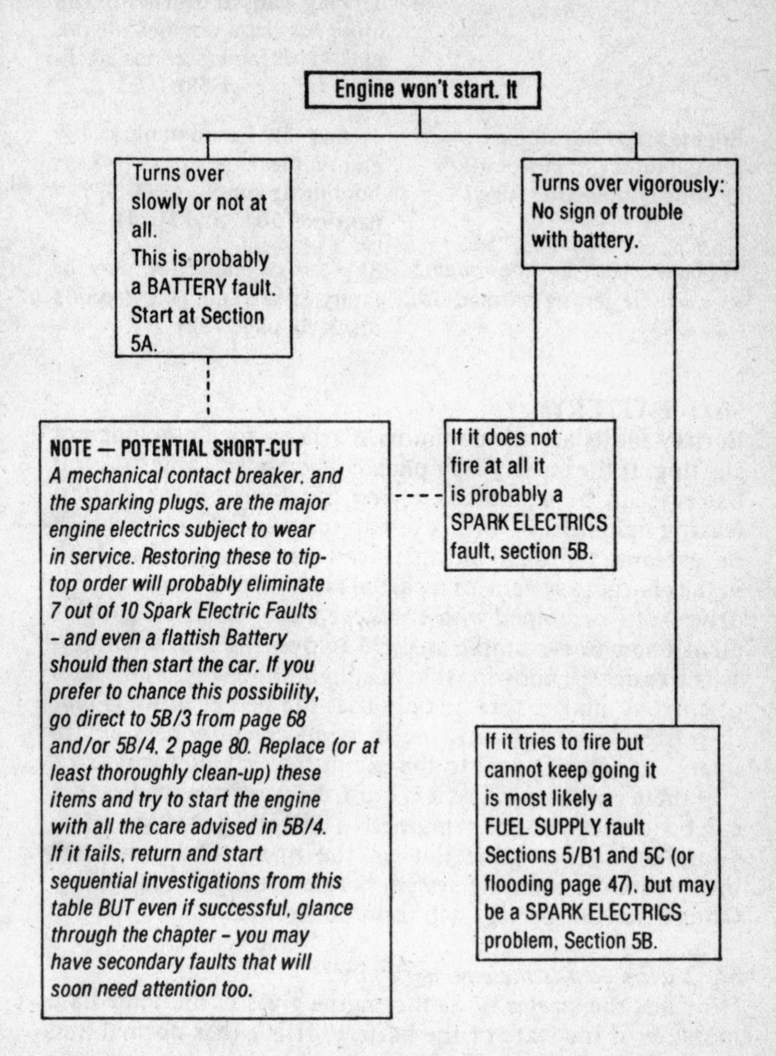

Table 1. Master Plan. Now turn to the appropriate section.

	2) Plug leads or distributor cap loose or less obvious SPARK ELECTRICS fault (sections 5B/1–5B/5 from page 58).
Engine starts but stops: 1) As you try to move off, or 2) shortly thereafter, or	1) and 2): Petrol tank nearly empty, leakage or blockage holding up supply. FUEL SUPPLY (sections 5B/1 and 5C/1).
3) later, just as the engine seems to be getting warmed-up.	3): Coil or capacitor may be faulty. SPARK ELECTRICS (section 5B/3, 5), page 75).

5A/1 BATTERY

Battery faults are the commonest reason for an engine not starting. If the battery is implicated, consider Table 2. A flat battery can be caused by trying too long on the starter, leaving lights etc. on (yes, even an interior light overnight!), or just failure through old age; it can also be caused by a fault in the charging system, or a partial fault there, such as a loose drive belt – combined with excessive use of electrical gadgets all at once. For example at night in pouring rain a battery-sensitive driver, knowing that headlights and wipers take a lot of current, makes sure he only uses the heater blower, rear de-mister, no. 2 (fast) speed windscreen wipers, extra intensity foglamps etc., to the extent that is vital for safety.

If there is a charging system fault, emergency remedies that can be undertaken are explained in Chapter 8, section 8B. If your battery has gone flat on the open road you must investigate the charging system before getting the car going. Otherwise your battery will soon be flat again!

5A/2 *How fast is the engine turning?*

How fast the starter turns the engine gives us an immediate measure of the state of the battery. It is either normal and energetic, or tired out (flat). It is possible (but comparatively remote) for a slow – "grinding" – starter, not to signal a flat battery but to be caused by loose connections to the starter, or by a fault in the starter motor itself. To avoid the chance of wearing down still further a battery that is nearly flat by

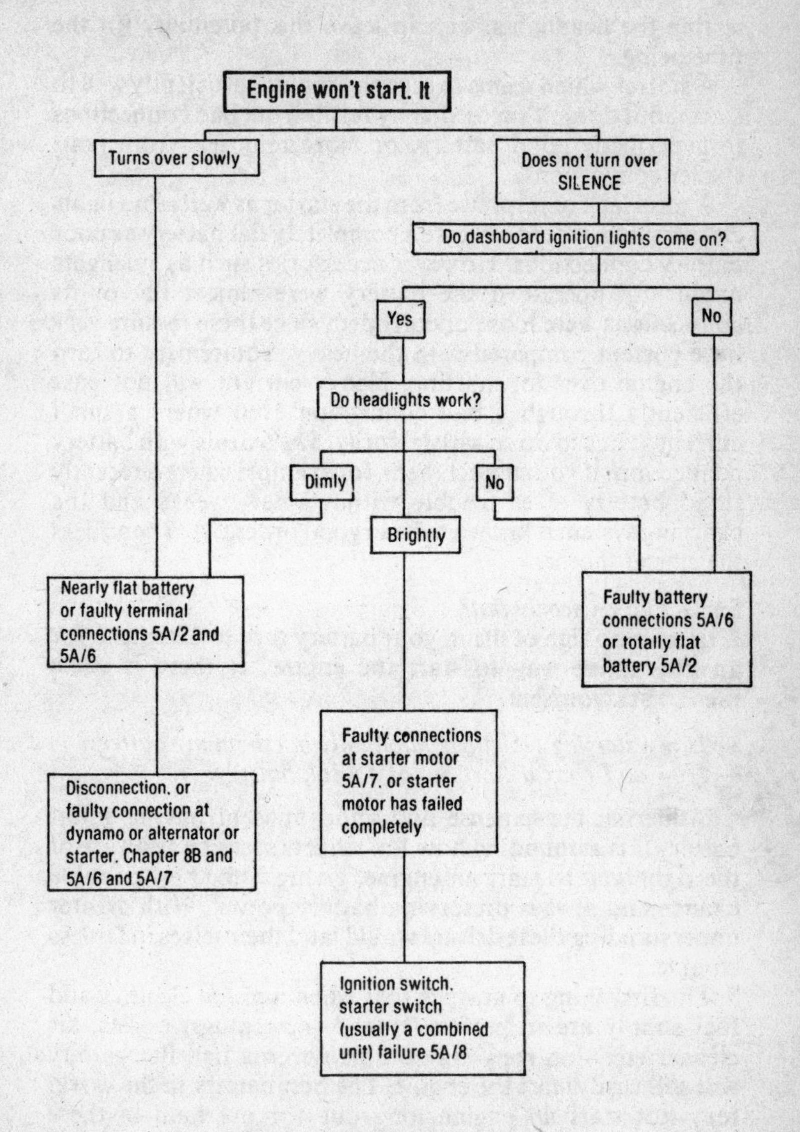

Table 2. BATTERY problems.

testing the headlights, we can leave this possibility for the time being.

A starter which seems to turn the engine sufficiently well to start it but doesn't succeed, may result from bad connections to a perfectly good battery, or more remotely from poor starter connections.

A total lack of response from the starter as well as no lights etc. working, would indicate a completely flat battery or poor battery connections. However accessories such as sidelights might still operate if the battery were almost flat or its connections were loose or corroded, since these require very little current compared with the heavy requirement to turn the engine over for starting. Heavy current will not pass efficiently through a bad connection even where a small current seems to do so satisfactorily. 5A/6 deals with battery connections if you suspect them, for example where a recently fitted battery gives trouble within a few weeks and the charging system is known to be in good order. 5A/7 considers the starter motor.

5A/3 *Flat or nearly flat?*

If there is no sign of life in your battery turn to Chapter 6 for an alternative way to start the engine. If there is some life . . . ask yourself:

Is my starting technique habitually harsh on my battery?
How do I coax a start out of a weak battery?

Considering the expense and annoyance of having a flat battery it is astounding how few drivers seem to be aware of the right way to start an engine, giving it the best possible chance and always preserving battery power. With greater understanding these drivers would land themselves in far less trouble.

The first thing to grasp is that when ignition electrics and fuel supply are in perfect "tune" (new plugs, points, air cleaner etc. – no ropy connections) even a half flat battery will still easily start the engine. The best battery in the world may not start an engine long due for overhaul in these departments. What is usually happening when an *engine won't go* easily, lies somewhere between these extremes; fuel and spark supply may be operating at say 60% efficiency, whilst the battery is 25% under power, or vice versa. Perhaps the engine is nearing service tune-up time, or some electrical connection is working itself loose; maybe the battery has not been looked after (see Chapter 17C, page 155), its connections are poor, or it is several years old, nearing the end of its life and unable to hold its charge for long; possibly the charging system no longer balances the demands upon it, with that vital bit to spare for re-charging the battery (see page 117 if you suspect this).

Whatever the situation, it will be made worse unless the engine is always started the right way. The final emergency, when the engine refuses to start, can be brought forward immeasurably otherwise.

In an ideal world, faced with the first sign of battery trouble, we would jump out and investigate on the lines described in this book before draining it further. With an ailing battery, a new set of mechanical contact breaker points and of sparking plugs, for example, might tip the balance in its favour. (And having got re-started, the first opportunity would be taken to have a garage run a check on all systems, and replace the battery if that were appropriate.) In the real world, whether the refusal to start has caught us away from home, or the car has been buried in a snowdrift since it was last used, the temptation instead is to grind away on the starter, exhausting the battery completely in the process.

If we do this without thought then, regardless of why the battery may have been dwindling in power, *there will come a point where the effort required by the battery to turn the engine leaves insufficient current to create a strong enough spark as well.* By the time the starter can only turn the engine with half its normal vigour, this point has probably been reached. It is senseless to continue. The time for investigation and/or immediate recourse to Chapter 6 for alternative ways to start has come. A push or tow start stands a good chance as long as the battery is not yet dead.

HOWEVER, BEFORE THAT STAGE, SUCH AN ENGINE CAN OFTEN BE COAXED INTO LIFE IF YOU KNOW HOW.

The right way to start an engine is always the same. When your battery is already weak it can mean success instead of failure:

5A/4 *Starting technique checklist*

* **Switch off ALL lights and electrical gadgetry**

Note especially the less obvious:
- rear window de-mister
- interior lights (shut doors, boot etc. so they are out!)
- de-mist blower
- high intensity rear foglights
- reversing light (works when gear lever in that position)

Before engine goes, refrain from operating:
- electric windows or sunshine roof
- radio/tape deck
- windscreen wipers
- cigar lighter
- footbrake (brakelights usually work even with ignition off)
- air conditioning

(Note: The most recent cars are "wired for idiots" so that every other item cuts out automatically whilst the starter is operated.)

* **Hold clutch pedal down**
(This saves the battery having to turn parts of clutch and gearbox.)

* **Use short (5-10 seconds maximum) bursts on starter: on fuel injected engines 15-20 second bursts are usually recommended.**

1. Allow 10 seconds between bursts as a rule.
2. In freezing weather, a longer rest (30 seconds – 1 minute) after the first burst, allows the battery more chance to recover from the effort of stirring the cold engine oil initially.

3. If it won't go after 10 attempts, wait 5–10 minutes before having one more series of tries; if it won't go then: a) if battery already low, turn to Chapter 6, b) if battery fine return to *clues for short cuts* page 39 and continue to investigate via this chapter from 5A/6 below.

BUT!

You may have a flooded engine, or have used too much choke initially. Check your maker's instruction handbook. It should give precise advice on avoiding this problem.

★ **Don't waggle your foot up and down on the accelerator absentmindedly between each try!**

Each press may be squirting neat petrol into the cylinders, flooding the engine.

COLD STARTS

1. a) If you have an automatic choke, hold your accelerator pedal *steady* ½–¾ down. (Note: Some automatic chokes require the slow flooring and release of the accelerator pedal once, before you attempt to start the engine – check your maker's instruction handbook).

b) Use a manual choke combined with accelerator pedal no more than ½ down – again, held steady.

2. After a whole series of tries (see above) it is possible the engine may be flooded. Push off a manual choke if fitted, *floor the accelerator*, and try several more bursts whilst holding the accelerator down. Should the engine suddenly try to fire, you may have put your toe on the trouble by clearing the excess fuel. Continue, and be ready to release the accelerator partially as soon as she goes. With a manual choke, be ready to pull it out again to keep the engine going once it has begun to fire.

HOT STARTS

1. A light touch held on the accelerator should be ample. Make sure a manual choke is fully pushed off.

2. If you think you may have flooded the engine with a careless toe, carry out no. 2 page 47 (except last sentence, which doesn't apply when hot).

5A/5 *Why is the battery flat?*
The main reasons for failure of this expensive item were set out in 5A/1/2/3, with protecting it from poor starting technique in 5A/4 above. Flattening the battery rapidly on the starter is the worst thing you can do to it. The battery will also become flat for a variety of other reasons including leaving sidelights on, leaving a door open so that the interior light was on, etc., as well as other "undiscoverable" reasons. Other than that, it will hold its charge long and well, and provided its electrolyte level is topped up regularly according to the maker's instructions, it should last from 3 to 5 years or more. If it does get flat it should be re-charged *slowly*. Using a

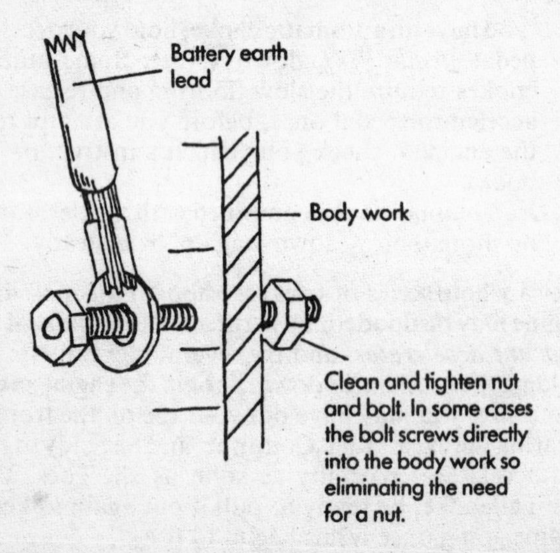

Fig. 17: The Battery Earth Connection to the Bodywork or Engine

trickle charger, or driving the car if it can be got going, is fine. Avoid the rapid boost charge some garages offer, which can be as damaging to the long term life of the battery as an idiot on the starter.

5A/6 *Battery connections*

What seems to be a nearly flat battery is frequently not the case at all. Poor connections will prevent starting. And, as noted on pages 40 and 44, loose battery connections may be implicated even though the starter turns the engine

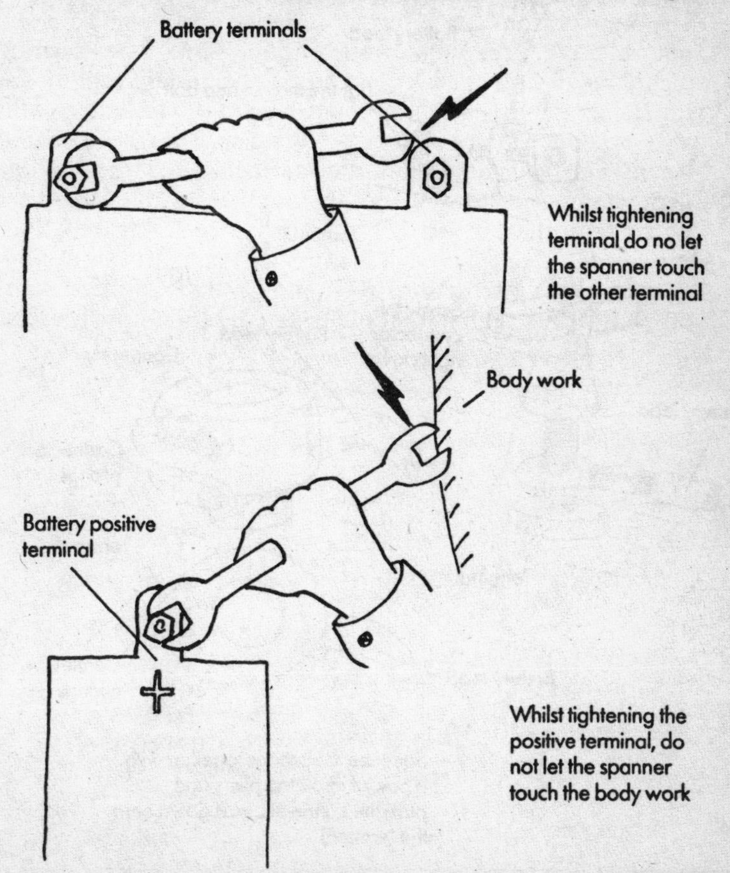

Fig. 18: Hazards of Tightening the Battery Terminal Connections

moderately well. They should always be checked before condemning other systems or the battery itself. If the positive terminal feels hot to touch this is a sure sign that a proper connection at the terminal is not being made.

Both terminals on top of the battery must be clean, free of corrosion, and done up tight – as must be the earth lead where it is bolted either to the bodywork or the engine block or gearbox. See figs. 17, 18 and 19.

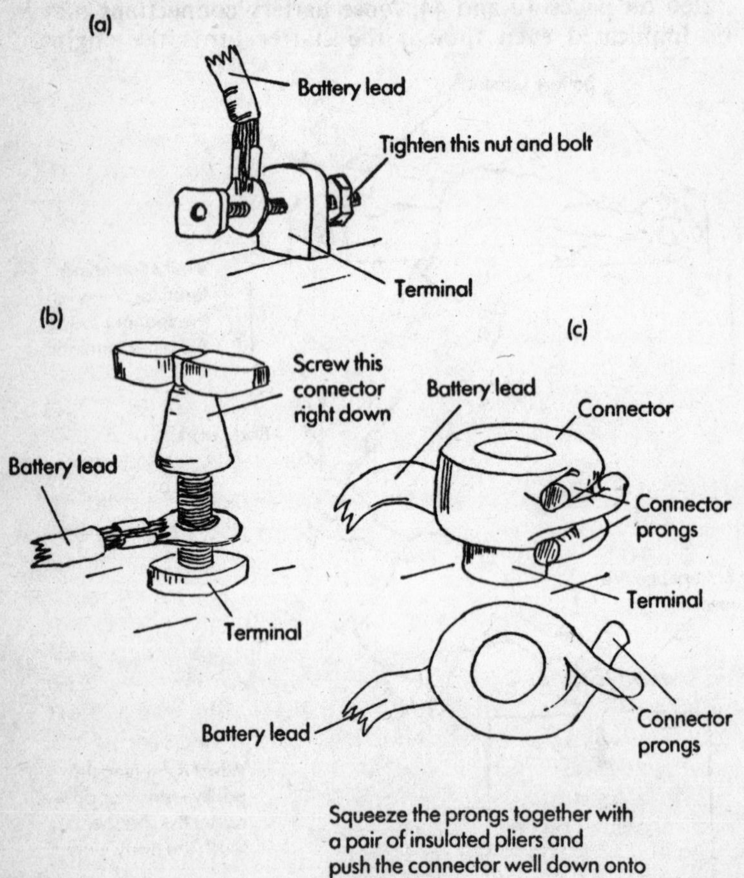

Fig. 19: Some Different Types of Battery Terminal Connectors

Undo each of these 3 connections in turn, remove verdigris, rust etc.; make sure metal contacts bright metal, and re-tighten them all soundly. A good tug on each lead held close to its connection – up, down or sideways – should not shift it at all. Be careful not to short-circuit the battery, giving yourself a fright and a shock (fig. 18). Incidentally, a little Vaseline smeared on the battery terminals before replacing and tightening them will help prevent corrosion.

There is a small chance that faulty wiring connections at the dynamo/alternator can prevent starting. They should be inspected as well.

WARNING: None of these battery, earth, or alternator connections must be disconnected when the engine is running. Doing so can wreck the alternator.

5A/7 *Battery or starter motor?*

As Table 3 reveals, with starter trouble the best place to look first is the battery and its connections (5A/1/2/3/5 and especially /6). Section 5A/2 hinted that trouble at the starter motor itself, when it will only turn the engine sluggishly or not at all, is much less likely. But it is next in line for our suspicions once you have O.K.'d the battery connections.

It may be jammed – and how you may succeed in unjamming it is explained below – or the connections to it may be ropy (also see below), or you may have a dud starter motor beyond the scope of this book.

When the engine turns grudgingly it is difficult to be certain initially, whether the trouble really is a failing battery or is at the starter motor. Your best *get you started* bet now, is to sidestep the starter motor and use an alternative way to start from Chapter 6. This avoids any chance of extinguishing the last drop of life in your battery.

For the righthand side of Table 3, you can return later to look over the starter motor connections or the possible need for starter motor overhaul (especially if jump leads to another battery didn't produce normal starter motor action, or there is no improvement after a run would have been expected to restore some life to the battery).

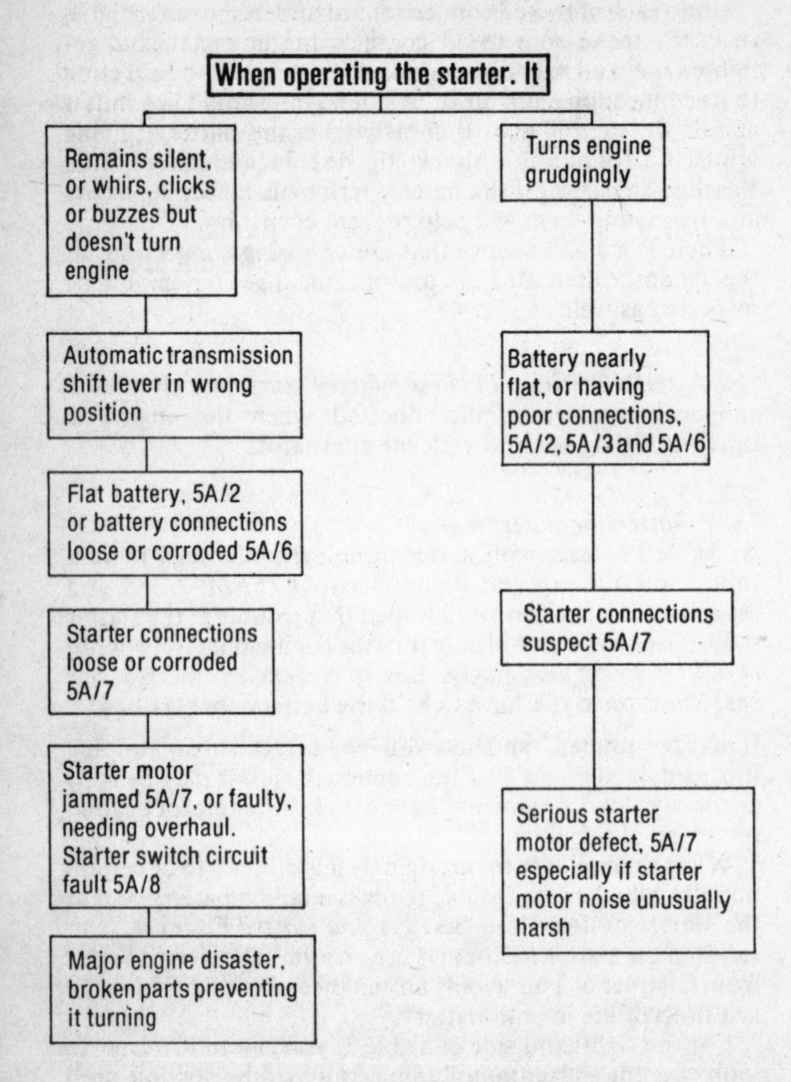

Table 3. Starter Motor Problems.

For the lefthand side of Table 3: 1) Silence, confirmed by lack of dashboard ignition lights, points hard at the battery; 2) Silence, *except* for a single click or "chonk" noise, could point to a jammed starter; or – very remotely – an engine locked from turning by broken major component(s).
3) A whir or buzz without turning the engine could be battery or starter trouble, or in the connections to either. Your best bets are:

for 1) Chapter 6, an alternative way to start.
for 2) See if headlights will come on brightly and remain so for a couple of minutes. If yes, look for a jammed starter as below; if you can't unjam it, a push or tow start is the only way.
If no, either of these or a jump-lead start (Chapters 6 and 10) should get you going.
for 3) Again an alternative start will be best, sorting out later why your battery is in trouble, or checking the starter motor and connections if they are still implicated.

Checking the starter connections
We have avoided this in our explanations so far, as they are usually buried deep in the engine compartment, (see page 35) and the choice of an alternative start has more appeal. However there is no harm in checking them at the same time as the battery connections; you may find a fault or reach a conclusion quicker. Figs. 20, 16 and 2 help you locate all the thick cable and thin wire connections to check out, both for tightness and bright metal to metal contact. Heed the warning on fig. 20!

Where a separate solenoid is fitted (inertia type starter), and the fault is in the solenoid, it may be possible to bypass the solenoid using a thick jump lead temporarily clipped across the 2 heavy cable connectors on the solenoid. You must use heavy cable for this to avoid undue sparking (ordinary thin wire could melt/burn out instantly). Make sure the car is out of gear and the ignition is switched off. Clip the lead to one terminal; holding the other end of the lead by the insulation you can then touch the other terminal long enough to see if the engine will turn over. Expect quite fierce sparking as you touch the terminal with the lead. If the starter motor now responds normally, you will be able to make the temporary connection again, with the ignition switched on so that the car can start. Alternatively some of these solenoids have a manual bridge facility. By pressing a rubber covered

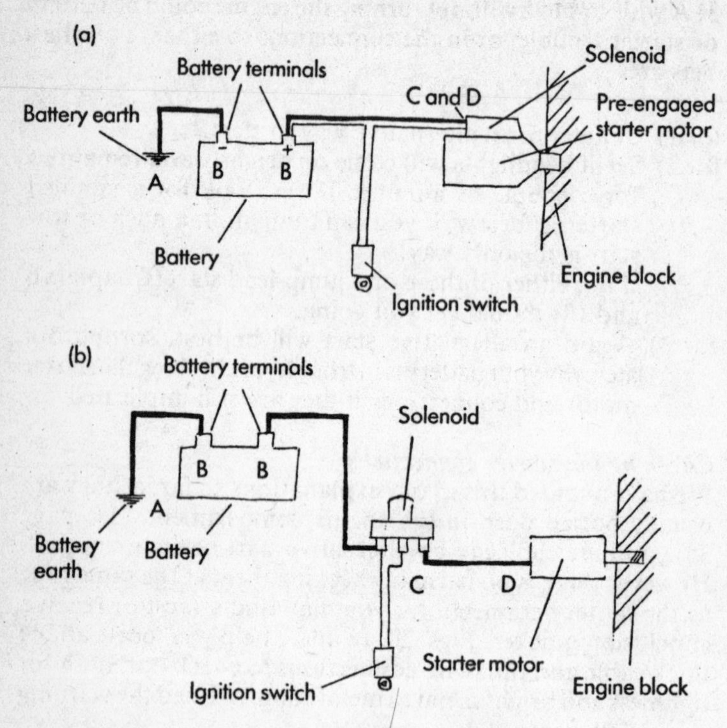

Fig 20: The Electrical Circuits for Pre-Engaged and Inertia-type Starter Motors
(a) Pre-engaged Starter Motor
(b) Inertia-type Starter Motor
Check out the electrical wiring:
A: Battery earth lead **B:** Battery terminals
C: Solenoid connections **D:** Starter motor connection(s)
WARNING: Disconnect the battery earth lead BEFORE checking solenoid or starter connections. Heavy (burn level) sparking and the possibility of the engine suddenly bursting into life will thus be avoided.

dome or a specially provided button in the middle of the unit the solenoid is activated just as it would be electrically by the ignition switch. Again if the solenoid has been the fault this will provide a means to start the car.

To unjam a jammed starter motor

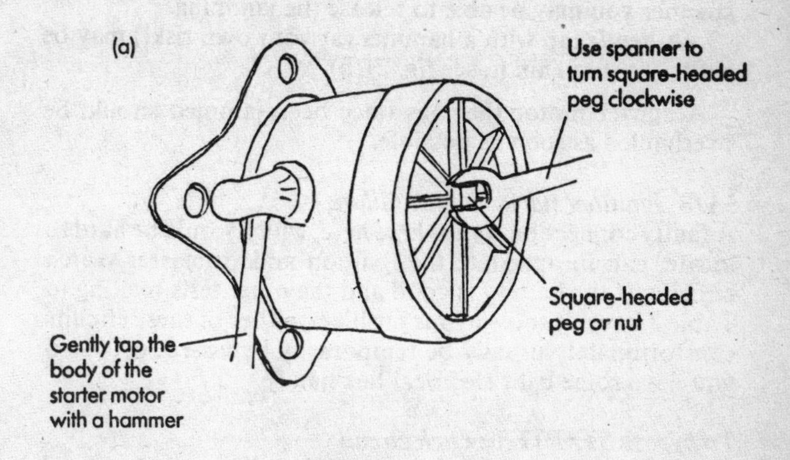

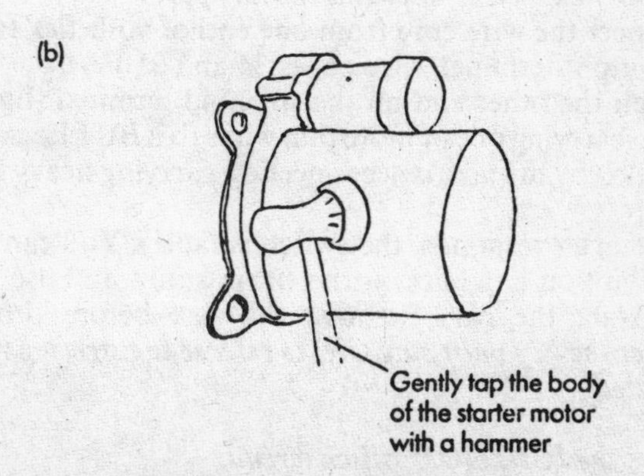

Fig 21: Freeing a Jammed Starter Motor
(a) Inertia-type Starter Motor
(b) Pre-engaged Starter Motor

Remove key from ignition switch:

1. (Not possible with automatic transmission.) Engage any gear (top may be easiest) and rock the car backwards and forwards, thereby shifting the engine rotation back and forth. You may free-up a modest jamming this way.
2. Some starters are fitted with a square-headed peg on the end of the starter motor as in fig. 21(a). If this will turn with a spanner you may be able to release the jamming.
3. A *gentle* tap with a hammer (at your own risk!) may be sufficient to unjam it, see fig. 21(b)

A starter motor that has once been jammed should be overhauled as soon as possible.

5A/8 *Ignition/starter switch failure*

A faulty connection somewhere here, which would be hard to locate, can incapacitate the ignition and/or starter switch circuits. If the battery is good and the other tests relating to Table 2 haven't solved your problem, either of these circuits can fortunately usually be temporarily bypassed, provided you have some light electrical flex handy.

To bypass STARTER switch circuit

SAFETY: *Put gear lever in neutral. Keep limbs, clothes – and the lighting flex – clear of engine moving parts:*

1. Connect the wire core from one end of your flex to the battery output terminal. (See pages 34 and 91.)
2. Touch the other end on the solenoid terminal (fig. 20, page 54) carrying one or more thin wires to it BUT be careful *not* to touch by mistake *any* connection carrying heavy thick cable.

If the starter responds, the switch is faulty. You can now put the ignition key back in the ON position and use your flex to start the car. Remove the flex before driving. *Remember the key must stay ON, to release the steering wheel lock if fitted.*

To bypass the IGNITION switch circuit:

1. Attach your flex to the battery as before. Attach other end to the coil terminal bearing the lead from the ignition switch (fig. 25, page 64).

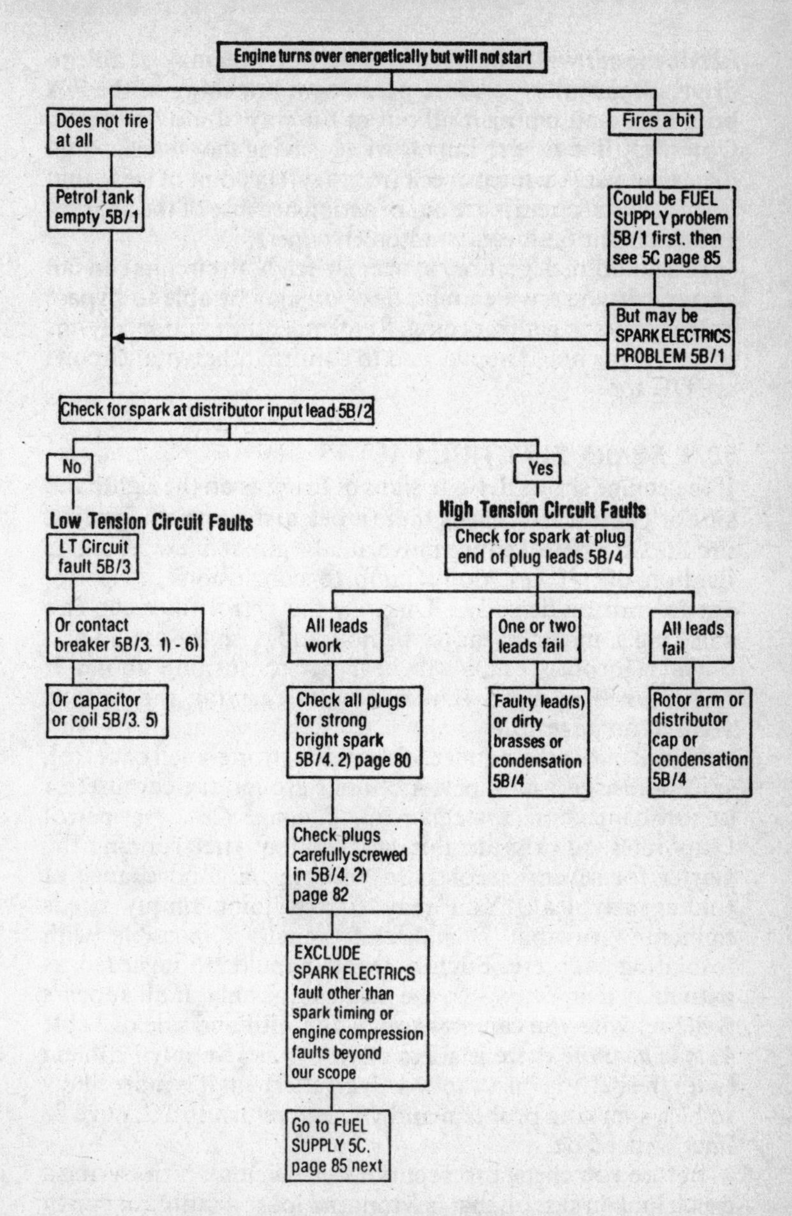

Table 4. SPARK ELECTRICS problems.

2. If the car will now start with the key, you may be able to drive, after making a more permanent attaching of the flex both ends and taping it all out of the way of moving parts. Obviously if it were to fall off while driving the engine would die. However you must check from a safety point of view, that no other vital circuits are out of action because of the ignition switch circuit fault e.g. windscreen wipers.

In a combined ignition/starter switch both circuits can fail at once. If you have enough flex you may be able to bypass both circuits to get you going. Remember the ignition key has to be ON, as noted above, and to confirm other vital circuits are OK too.

5B/1 SPARK ELECTRIC FAULTS

If the engine shows definite signs of firing as on the righthand side of Table 4, first check there is petrol in the tank. Ignition on: does the petrol gauge move at all? (give it a few seconds): ignition off. If yes, don't jump to conclusions . . . petrol gauges can be defective. Unscrew the petrol filler cap (no smoking!), put your ear to the hole and push the car up and down vigorously. You will hear petrol sloshing about. If not . . . walkies time! (Unless you're carrying the can, as advised on page 15.)

Check under the bonnet. If there is a strong smell of petrol, sniff on. Inspect all pipework/joints around the carburettor or fuel injection systems (fig. 8, page 26). As petrol evaporates quickly, do this immediately after running the starter for several seconds so you have a good chance of finding any leak. You may find a joint simply needs tightening or that a makeshift repair is possible with insulating tape etc. Such a repair should be regarded as extremely temporary – to the next garage only. If all appears well fuel-wise you can now follow the left-hand side of Table 4. It is *possible* there is a less obvious Fuel Supply Problem (with the betting on a choked air cleaner) but it is more likely to be a sparking problem and you can return to 5C, page 85 later, if need be.

Before you check for a spark as below, it's worth having a quick look in case all that is wrong is a loose distributor cap or plug lead(s) that have come off.

5B/2 *Check for a spark*
When there are *no* signs of the engine firing, FIRST check for petrol in the tank as just described. Assuming you have petrol, your first objective is to establish as below, whether there is a good High Tension spark reaching the distributor input lead from the coil. Table 4 will then lead you on to the YES, HT circuit checks, or to the NO, LT circuit checks accordingly.

But first a small diversion . . . If along the YES route, dampness/condensation is an obvious culprit, tackle that first. A high tension spark is especially prone to be diverted via moisture or accumulated oily gunge covering the HT leads and connections – including anywhere along the one from the coil. *Damp inside* the distributor cap will jinx things too. An anti-condensation spray, said to drive water away, is available (Chapter 2) but the best approach is to mark the plug leads so you will know which is which, and remove the distributor cap from the car with these leads attached, (see page 68 if need). For this purpose undo the HT lead from the coil at the distributor end; it may have a screw collar, or it may simply pull off.

All traces of moisture or dirt must now be removed from the cap and leads. The lead from the coil should also be attended to – still in situ, in the car. Be thorough, till every piece is clean and dry. Wipe clean/dry the white ceramic insulators of the plugs too, before putting everything back. That should be enough to get you started if damp has been the major problem.

Once damp can be eliminated here is how you check for the HT spark reaching the distributor input properly.

Safety: Before any HT spark test look round for any petrol leakage – especially if there is any strong smell of petrol. Remember that the invisible vapour can catch light instantaneously.

1. Make sure the car is in neutral (*essential*) and handbrake is *on*.
2. Unscrew (or pull off as appropriate) at the distributor, the input HT lead that comes from the coil. Check that the other end is still firmly attached at the coil. See figs. 5, 23, 36 and 37; holding the lead just above the sleeve, it

should not be possible to push it any further down towards the coil.
Using *insulated* pliers to avoid getting a shock, hold the bared distributor end of this lead about 5mm (the thickness of a pencil) from the engine block.
Activate the starter for several seconds, with the ignition on if that has a separate switch. A steady stream of bright, blue-tinged, sparks should arc (spit with a crack) across from the end of the lead to the engine block. You may have to shade the area from bright sunlight to see but the sparking obtained must be continuous and of good fierce quality whilst the lead is held the right distance from the block. This is the basic procedure but the less initiated may need some further tips.

First, the end of the HT lead may not immediately reveal any metal core or contact to hold that 5mm from the engine block just described. Because of a sleeved end, designed to hold the lead in place, you may find the electrical contact point is hidden well up inside there. Some types can be slid back to access the metal contact and this should be done in order to investigate the spark. In others this proves impossible and a makeshift extension such as a paper-clip is needed. You can get the idea from figs. 22 and 23.

Second, you may need *two* people – one to hold the lead and observe the spark and one to operate the starter. Some older cars can be started at the solenoid as described on page 54. Most can't. However, if you are on your own, all may not be lost. Bind the HT lead to a convenient structure with

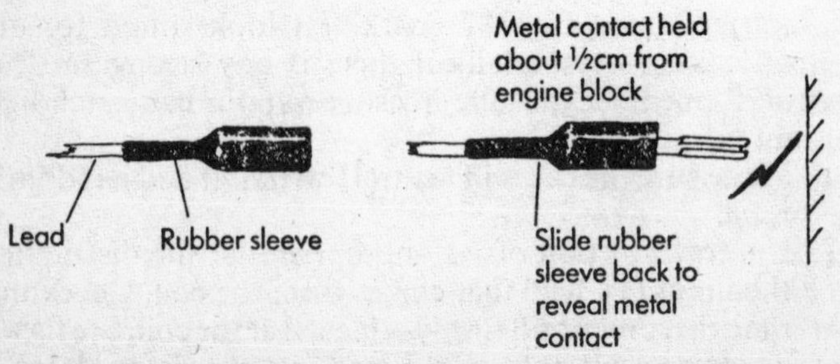

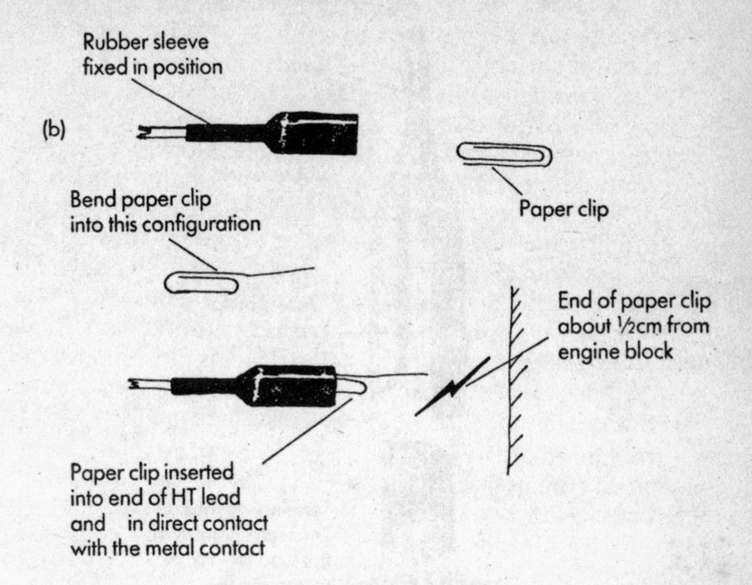

Fig. 22: Tips for Testing for a Spark at the End of HT leads
(a) HT Leads where the Rubber Sleeve Slides Back
(b) HT Leads where the Rubber Sleeve Does Not Slide Back

string or tape, so that the end is held at the right arc-ing distance from the engine block. With one hand on the ignition/starter switch, peek round the edge of the bonnet as in fig. 24. The test should be possible without you getting too contorted.

Alternatively, if you have a jump lead you can bypass the starter switch. Attach one end to the heavy cable *terminal* at the starter. (There should be no need to undo the permanent cable.) Remember you will need the ignition switch on when ready. To operate the starter as required, simply touch the other end of the jump lead on the output terminal of the battery (see pages 34 and 91). Hold the jump lead by the insulated part to avoid any shock as there will be some sparking. N.B. Do *not* attach the jump lead to the battery first, thinking it will then be easier to touch the starter terminal; you would be holding a live heavy voltage cable which could spark dangerously against almost anything

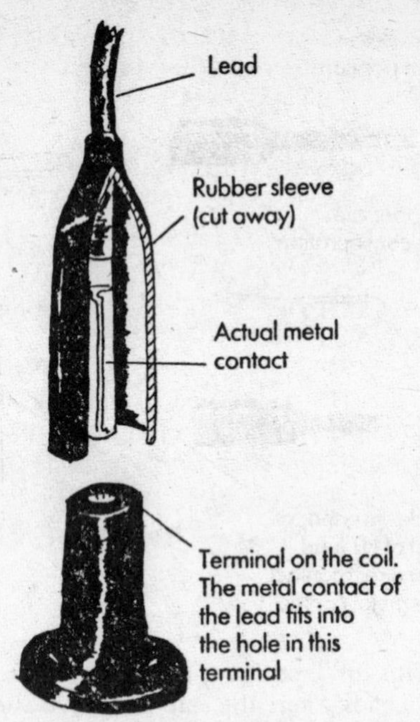

Fig. 23: Cut-Away View of an HT Connection at the Coil
The metal contact is screwed into the inner core where carbon-filled leads are used; where a wire-stranded core is used there is an obvious means used to ensure a good electrical connection with the metal contact.

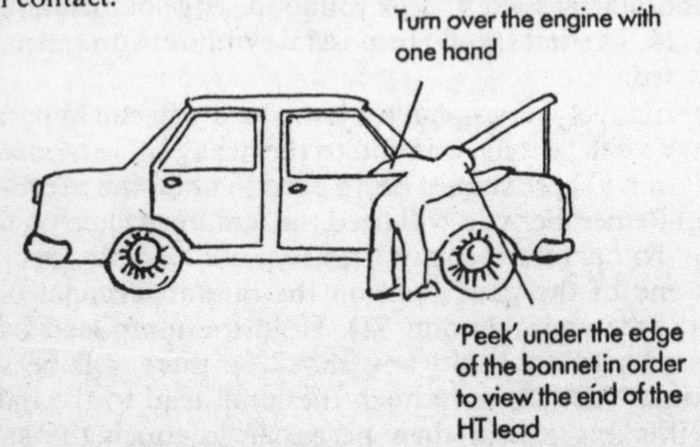

Fig. 24: Testing for a Spark in the Ignition System with Only One Person (provided you can reach the ignition/starter switch).

getting in its way. Do not use thinner cable; as it will not carry the current, it could burn – including your hands!

Spark test result
If there is a strong bright spark stream *at the correct distance from* the block, as described above, the coil and LT circuits are in good order; follow Table 4, YES, starting at 5B/4.

If there is no spark stream, or merely a feeble or intermittent one, check the battery connections (see page 49) then follow Table 4, NO, beginning below.

If none of the above test methods are possible, a partial test may point you in the right direction. Flicking contact breaker points open as described below, should produce a single HT spark on to the engine block in the way described above, each time. You won't know if there would be a good stream but at least you will know whether you are getting anything at all.

5B/3 *Low tension circuit check*
For the first test below, turn to page 68 and figs 28 and 29 – should you need to find out how to get at a contact breaker and make sure the points are closed.

If flicking open the contact breaker points (mechanical contact breakers only) with a pencil or anything non-conductive whilst the ignition is *on*, produces a small but visible spark across the points this shows current is reaching them; you can assume your trouble is *at the points* rather than elsewhere in the LT circuit. Move directly to page 66, Contact Breaker Points. Incidentally, an unusually vibrant spark here, may be a clue that your capacitor is not absorbing excess electricity as it should. See page 75.

If you *don't get* such a spark – or if you have electronic ignition which rarely itself fails – look at the rest of the low tension wiring as below first.

The low tension circuit wire connections are depicted in fig. 25. Unfortunately they cannot all be got at too easily. The circuit runs from the battery output terminal via the ignition switch, through the coil (C to C) to the distributor body at E. Inside the body it reaches the contact breaker points (or electronic ignition, Chapter 4, page 22) housed there, and is then completed to earth via the distributor body base.

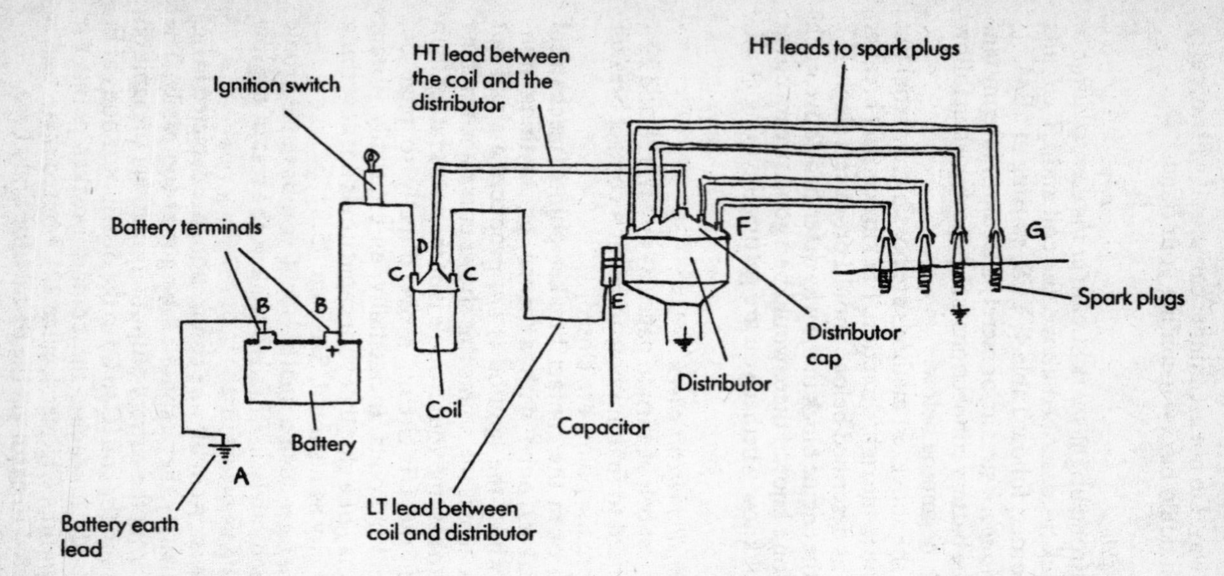

Fig. 25: The Ignition System Circuit and the Areas of Common Faults
Most capacitors are mounted within the distributor body, as in fig. 6. On Electronic systems no separate capacitor is required.

Any connection in this circuit that is loose or comes apart simply by tugging gently, has to be suspect. Chaffed or broken wires must be rectified. The vital importance of having both battery terminals as well as the earth/body contact A, clean and tight, is explained from page 49, so attend to those first. Provided the ignition warning light comes on, a fault at the switch is unlikely. (You could bypass the switch as a last resort - see page 56.) Check both connections C at the coil, and then E at the distributor for cleanness and tightness (E may be at the edge, or inside under the distributor cap – see page 68 for removal, and fig. 6, page 24). The distributor body cannot fail to be earthed.

Work thoroughly. Although doubtful connections can simply be tightened up or pushed together, depending on type, to be certain of a 100% electrically sound connection it is always best to take them fully apart. You can then ensure there will be good metal-to-metal contact by rubbing each part with emery paper or scraping with a screwdriver blade and finishing with a clean cloth or old toothbrush. Make certain a screw type reconnection is tight or that a spade type makes a firm sliding fit. See fig. 26.

Finally, make sure that the screw securing the capacitor to the distributor body (which doubles as the earth contact) is tight, and that the contact connecting it to the points is also sound. See figs. 6, 32 and 33, and for removing the distributor cap, 1) on page 68.

Damaged LT wires

A chaffed or broken wire may divert a spark away from its intended target. Chaffed insulation can be bound with insulating tape or even Elastoplast. A broken wire should be replaced with a similar grade of wire but in an emergency you can attempt to fix it. If the break is close to one end it may be possible to reattach the wire to the connector (see fig. 27) but if the break is in the middle this cannot be done. However, you might be able to interleave and twist such wires together and bind them with insulating tape. Such a temporary joint must be replaced with a proper "in line" connector (available from motorists' DIY stores etc.) as soon as possible.

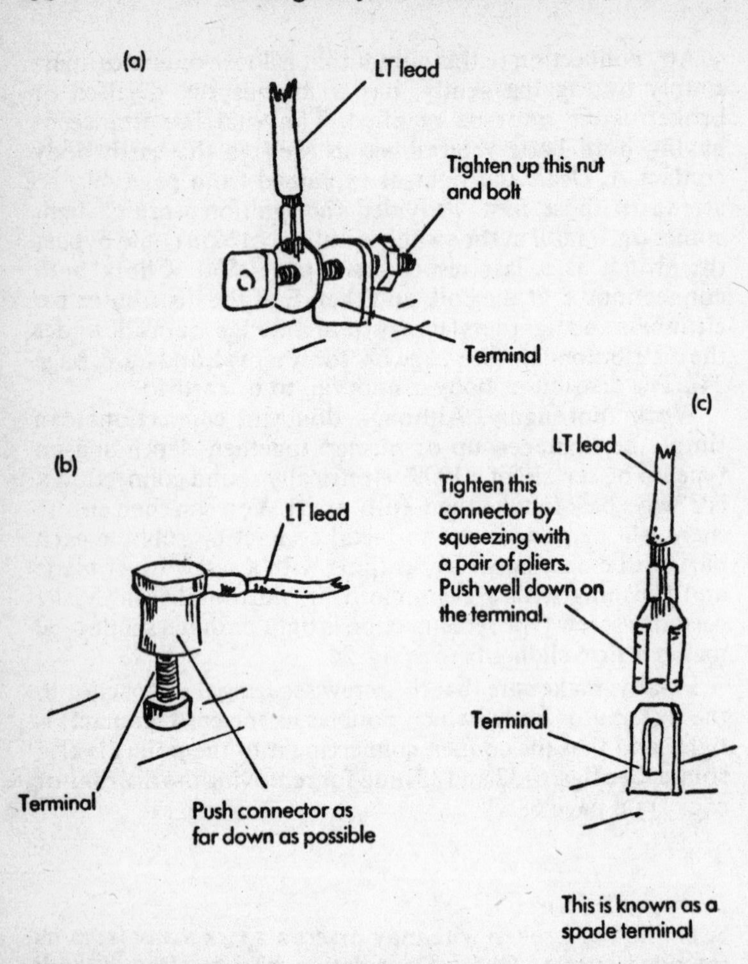

Fig 26: The Different Types of LT Circuit Connections and Push-On Connectors at the Coil Terminals.

The contact breaker points
If all the above connections and wires seem O.K. the only trouble spot left in the LT circuit is in the mechanical contact breaker. These being subject to wear, one can see why contact-less electronic ignition is a great advantage.

The points either "burn out" or the essential gap set between the electrodes goes adrift. Having the wrong gap affects the timing as well as the quality of the High Tension spark which the coil (fed by this LT circuit) can produce – and

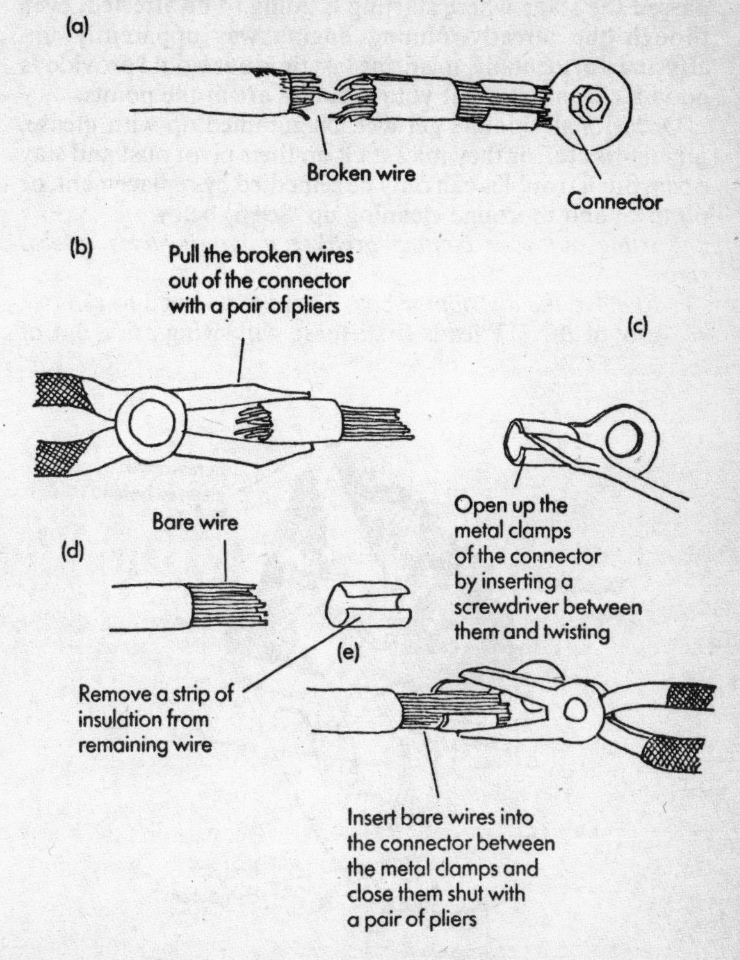

Fig. 27: The Reconnection of a Broken Wire
Should the connector chance to snap, the wire can be twisted directly round the terminal under its nut, or possibly even bound on securely with insulating tape.

hence engine starting. It should also be emphasised that points problems mostly develop whilst the engine is running. Although the engine may have appeared to run well last time out, gradual deterioration in points' performance may have passed the stage where starting is going to be affected, even though the already-running engine was apparently unaffected. Incidentally, misfiring last time out would provide as good a clue as any that your troubles are at the points.

Occasionally points get wet, or gummed up with grease, oil, debris etc., or they may stick on their pivot post and stay open. Such troubles can only be remedied by replacement, or removal and thorough cleaning up. See 6) below.

Sorting out your contact breaker points involves several steps:

1. *Remove the distributor cap.* There is no need to remove any of the HT leads first; these will swing aside out of

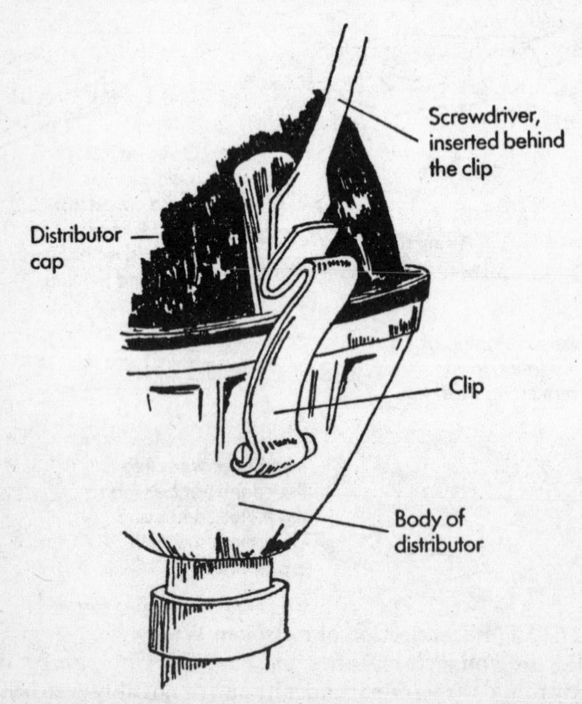

Fig. 28: Undoing the Clips that Hold on the Distributor Cap.

your way with the cap. If you are unsure about refitting it the right way round, first place a chalk mark on the cap and a corresponding mark on the distributor body. Aligning these marks will ensure correct refitting. The cap is held on by 2 metal clips, one on each side; these are easiest undone by a screwdriver blade behind them (see fig. 28), to act as a lever. **WARNING!** Notice as you remove the cap whether any locating lugs will have to engage at the join when it goes back. The plastic could be broken the instant the starter turns if the cap does not settle back snugly in the correct position.

2. *Remove the rotor arm* which simply slides up off the central spindle or cam (see fig. 35, page 77). Put it somewhere safe, since a rotorless engine is useless. (If you wish to leave your car for some time and are worried about having it stolen, removing the rotor will foil the casual car thief. Remember it when you come back and don't "sit on the starter" wondering why it won't go!)
3. With the rotor arm removed you can now *examine the contact breaker points* which are below. They will probably be closed but you will need to get them in the open position. The points open when the "heel" (shown in fig. 29) has been pushed the maximum amount by one of the lobes on the cam (see also fig. 6, page 24). The open position can be achieved in several ways:

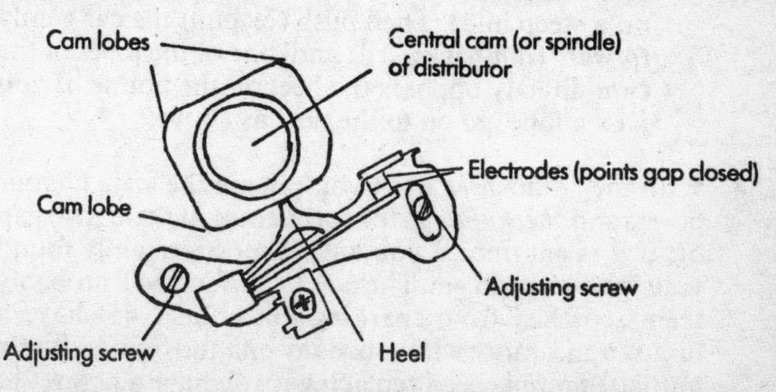

Fig. 29: (a) Contact Breaker Points gap closed

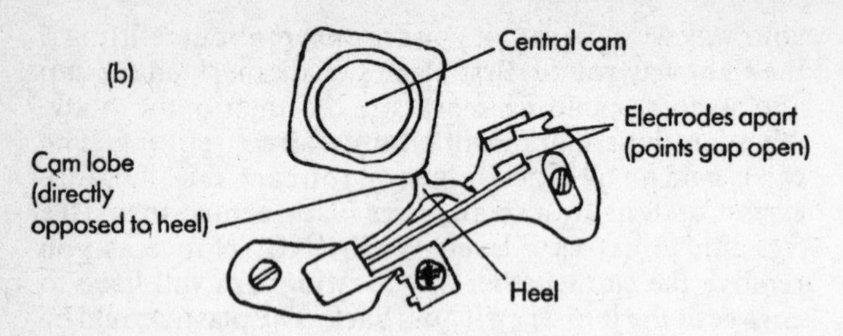

Fig. 29: (b) Contact Breaker Points gap open

Either place the car in neutral with the handbrake *on* and then, taking a firm grip on the drive belt, rotate it *clockwise* (see fig. 30) so that the cam also rotates – stopping it when the *top* of one of the lobes of the cam has reached the heel on the points (see fig. 29). Do not turn back to get it right. Go on to the next lobe, arriving by clockwise turning of the drive belt. Take care. This does require a bit of strength and there is some risk of damaging your knuckles in the process. Removing the sparking plugs (see page 81) releases engine compression and makes it easier.

A second and easier technique – unfortunately no use with automatic transmission – is to select top gear and release the handbrake (*not* to be attempted on a steep hill!). Then push (or pull) the car gently *forward* (not backward) until one of the lobes of the cam directly opposes the heel on the points. If you pass a lobe, go on to the next as above.

4. With the points now open you can see the state of your points and *check the gap* for correctness. If there is no gap or, if it is enormous, you have almost certainly found your ignition problem. The points' surfaces will probably seem scorched from sparking but should not have a lumpy appearance with too many pits and bumps. Badly mutilated points need replacing if you have a new set to hand, or, at the least, taking out and rubbing as smooth

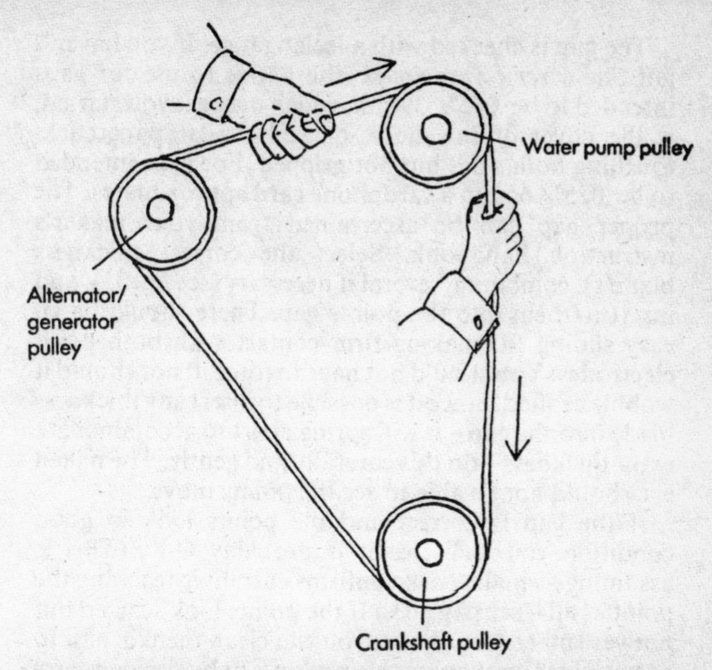

Fig. 30: Rotating the Distributor Cam via Using the Drive-Belt

as possible with emery paper, or on a matchbox side or paving stone, to effect a temporary repair. If all looks well you may only need to check the gap as explained next. Otherwise, for removing the points and/or re-setting the gap, go on to 5) below.

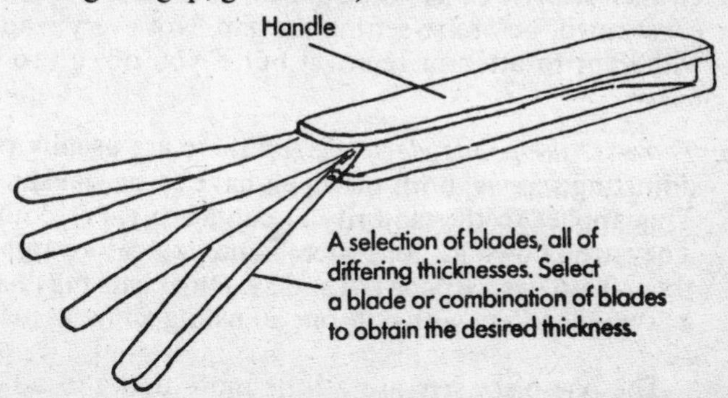

Fig. 31: Feeler Gauge

The gap is checked with a feeler gauge. If you haven't got one a *very, very rough* alternative to use for gaps intended to be .015"/.39mm, which may get you started, is the cover of this book or any similar paperback, touching both sides but not gripped. For gaps intended to be .025"/.65mm a cardphone card approximates. The proper gap can be ascertained from your maker's instruction handbook. Select the correct thickness blade(s), combining several if necessary (see fig. 31), and insert it/them into the points gap. There should be an easy sliding fit, making firm contact with both point electrodes. You should not have to force it, nor should it wobble around. Since it is possible to insert any thickness blade into the gap – it will spring apart to accommodate extra thickness – do this carefully and gently. The naked eye should not be able to see the points move.

If the gap is correct and the points look in good condition your LT circuit is probably O.K. (This is assuming a small spark confirms current is reaching the point at all – see page 63.) If the points look scarred but not yet ruined (see above) you can clean them in situ to some degree, perhaps with a penknife or by sliding emery paper or a matchbox side between them while they are closed. They should then be re-set as in 5) below. Finally, blow away all specks of dust etc.

If the points are in bad shape, or any trace of oil, grease or water has got on to them, they are best taken out to be cleaned really well as noted above, or to have new ones substituted, before re-setting the gap. Not every reader will want to attempt removal but if you do, go to 6) below.

5. *To re-set the points electrode gap* there are usually two adjusting screws, both of which have to be slackened. This applies to the majority of contact breaker points. They are known as "one-piece" and you can recognise them from figs. 6 (page 24) and 29. Older cars may have a "two-piece" set with only one adjusting screw, as in fig. 32.

   The one-piece sets are a little more tricky to adjust because they are spring-loaded. Whichever type you

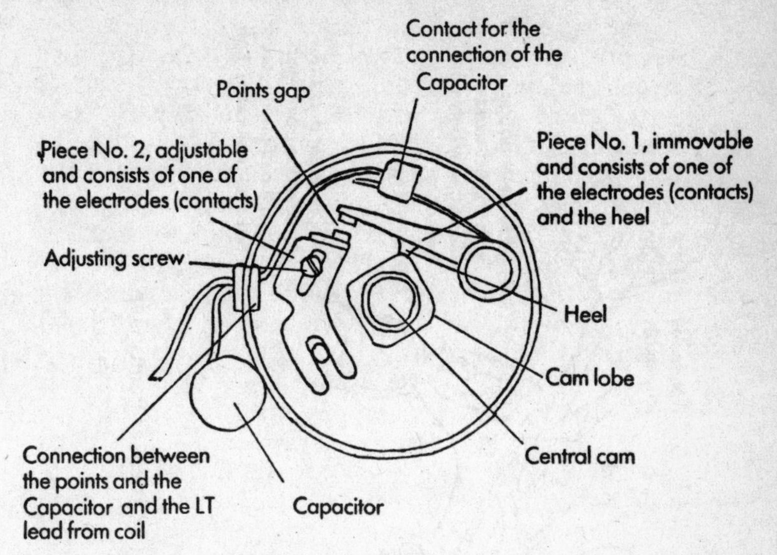

Fig. 32: Internal View of a Distributor with a "Two-Piece" Contact Breaker Points Set
Compare this view with the internal view of a distributor with a "one-piece" contact breaker points set as presented in fig. 6. Many cars have the capacitor inside the distributor housing; this view shows an externally located one.

have, first rotate the cam so that the heel is atop one of the lobes as explained in 3) above. Now slacken off both adjustment screws of a one-piece set or the single adjustment screw on a two-piece set. Loosen the screw(s) just enough for the movable point to be able to shift. Find the position when the screw(s) is/are just "pinch-tight" (on the "one-piece" the screw furthest from the point can be fully slackened – no. 2, fig. 33).

Open or shut the points as required to achieve the sliding fit already just described in 4), of the correct-sized feeler gauge blade(s). Either do this with your finger, or, if a screwdriver adjustment slot is provided, turning the screwdriver blade in the slot provides ideal leverage. Remove the feeler gauge, maintain the gap by finger pressure with a free hand, and using the *correct*-sized screwdriver, tighten up the adjustment screw(s). They

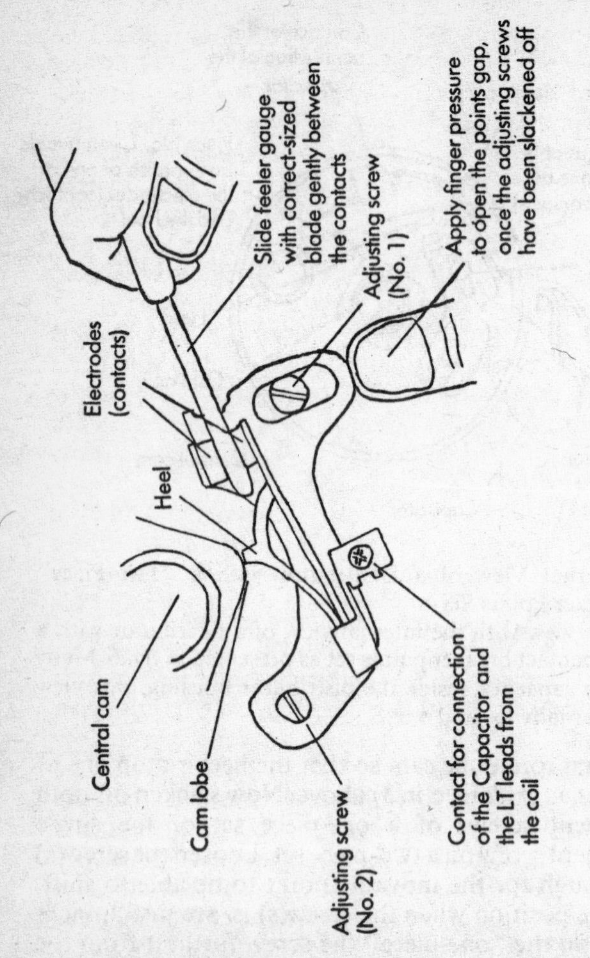

Fig. 33: Adjusting the Contact Breaker Points Gap.

need to be tight but don't overdo it and strip the threads or burr the top of the screw.

When the screw(s) is/are fully tightened, re-check the points gap. If it is wrong repeat the procedure. Practice makes perfect!

Replace the rotor arm and distributor cap. Make sure the keyway on the rotor locates fully home in its slot on the cam; ensure the distributor cap has the correct snug fit (see page 69).

Other than fitting new points if you choose to do so, for which see 6) below, you have done all you can by way of checking the LT circuit, along the NO route of Table 4. You will either now have a good HT spark and the engine will start if there are no other problems compounding your trouble, or you have a faulty capacitor, a faulty coil, or (remotely) a duff HT lead between the coil and the distributor (see 5B/4, 1), page 79).

Unfortunately there is no really satisfactory way to know whether a capacitor is taking up unneeded current as it should; if the points have worn out very quickly from excessive sparking (under 5,000 miles) this is an indication, unless an incorrect points gap has been the cause. It is best if a suspect capacitor is replaced but your attention to the points ought to get you going for the time being even with an ineffective capacitor.

A defective coil is *very* unusual – there are no moving parts. The only way to be sure if it is faulty is to fit a replacement. If that solves your problem you can enjoy smashing the old one up with a hammer, if necessary for your emotional health!

6. *Fitting* new *contact breaker points* or replacing cleaned-up ones is easy, provided you are utterly observant when you remove the points earlier. Anyone reasonably nimble-fingered with Meccano or Lego should be competent. The key thing to understand is that the correct electrical pathway depends on all the little plastic insulators, wires and suchlike, going back exactly whence they came. Without that there will be a short-circuit, not dangerous but robbing you of the chance to start the car until an expert can reassemble the points correctly. Draw yourself a blown-up picture as you take the suspect set out, if that helps.

Whether you have a one or two-piece contact breaker set, it can be seen that the parts all sit on a metal base, and that they are hinged or held on a threaded post, or two posts one of which may not be threaded. The pieces to come off and the wires to disconnect can be lifted from their respective post(s) once the nuts and adjusting screw(s) have been removed

With the new set or the cleaned-up points back in place, re-set the points gap as in 5) above.

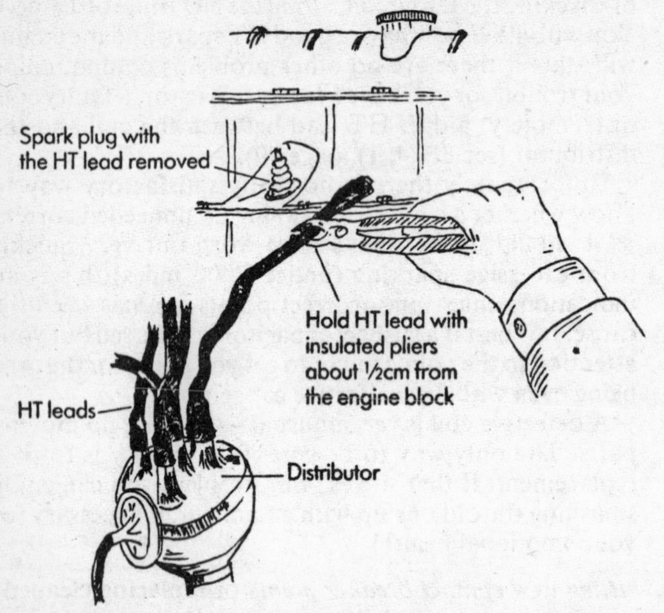

Fig 34: **Testing for a Spark Through the HT Leads to the Spark Plugs**

5B/4 ***High Tension Circuit Check***

This section *assumes a good HT spark stream* at the distributor end of the HT lead from the coil as detailed in the test in section 5B/2, page 59. Fit that lead back into the distributor cap, and the cap on to the distributor if it has been removed.

The HT sparks have to arrive along that lead and pass along the rotor arm out to the plugs in turn (in the firing order of the engine), whence they earth through the engine block after igniting the fuel. See fig. 25, page 64.

The next step is to discover whether the sparks reach each sparking plug satisfactorily. If not there is a fault in the rotor arm or in its brush or arm connection to the input lead (fig. 35) or in the output connections, or the HT leads to the plugs themselves. The output connections include the peripheral

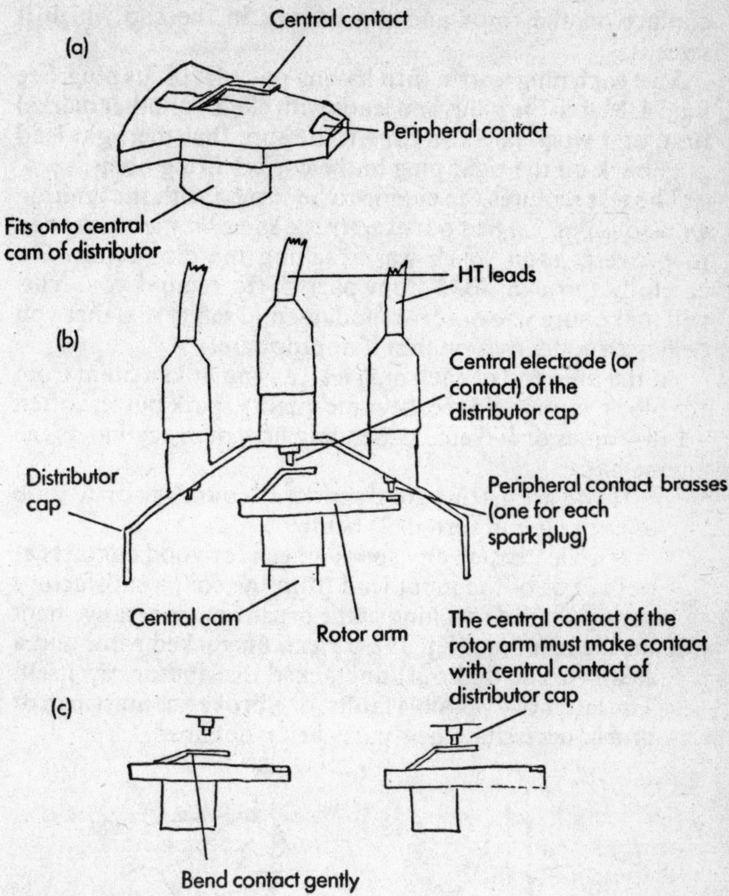

Fig. 35: Rotor Arm
(a) External View (b) Cut-away View of Rotor Arm in Position
(c) Electrical Contact. Bend this up gently if required. Use emery paper/matchbox side etc. to shine up this and central electrode in cap for good electrical contact.

Sometimes a spring-loaded carbon brush in the distributor cap replaces the central electrode shown, as well as the contact *arm* on the rotor. The brush in this case must press on to the centre top of the rotor arm when the distributor cap is in place. Check that the spring-loading has not stuck. Shine up metal top of rotor arm.

contact on the rotor and the brasses in the cap which it sweeps.

Test each plug lead in turn having pulled it off its plug. See fig. 34. Match the plugs and leads with chalk (or other marks) first, and work one-at-a-time to be sure that the right lead goes back on the right plug in the correct firing order.

The test requires the engine to be turned with the ignition *on*, and is best carried out *exactly* the same way as you tested to prove a good spark was reaching the distributor. Go carefully through 5B/2 from page 59 to remind you. This will make sure you observe fundamental safety and that you deal with condensation first if appropriate.

At the plug end of each plug lead as you hold it 5mm from the block you should see the same quality spark but less often - 1 in 4 times or 1–6 etc., depending how many cylinders the engine has:-

If you are getting good sparks all round, go on to look at each plug in turn in 2) below.

If *all* leads lack any spark, check for good contacts at both ends of the input lead from the coil, a satisfactory spring-loaded touching of the brush or arm arrangement on the rotor (see fig. 35), a clean uncracked rotor and a clean (inside and out) uncracked distributor cap itself. The latter two possible faults, or a broken contact arm or brush, necessitate new parts being obtained.

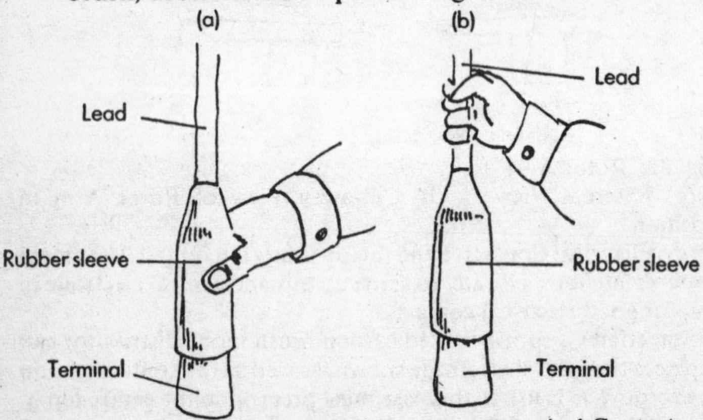

Fig. 36: The Correct Way to Ensure Sound Electrical Contact with HT Leads

If *some* leads, but not all, produce no spark, look at the output connection(s) at the distributor, and scrape off any burn marks at the peripheral contact on the rotor or on the brass contact(s) concerned inside the cap (fig. 35). Emery paper is the ideal thing to give the clean, bright metal-to-metal finish required but you may have to find a substitute. Any burn marks or black zig-zaggy marks inside the cap leading away from any brass, should be scratched away as far as possible. The plastic cap body should be shiny and clean inside throughout.

Should this improve things a new cap, and/or rotor arm if badly worn, will be needed shortly but you may get home.

It is possible for a plug lead to fail internally within its carbon filling, or through chaffing, or because of the metal end-contacts not piercing far enough into the carbon – or when end-contacts are not soundly connected to the wire strands of a wire-core lead. Check the leads as in 1) below if you suspect this.

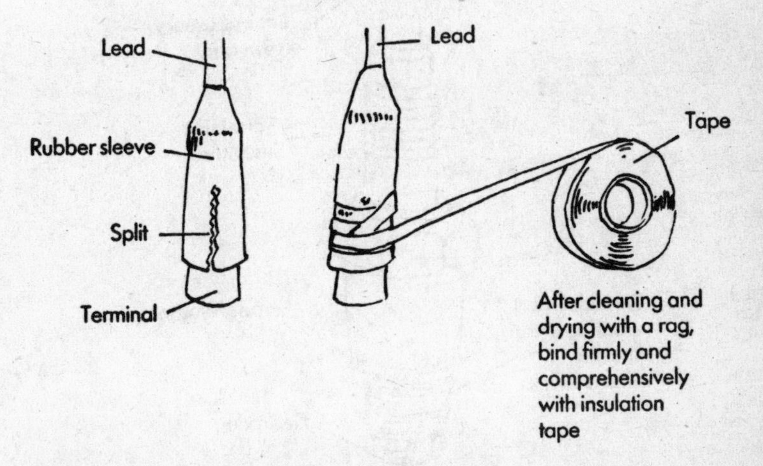

Fig 37: Temporarily Repairing a Split Rubber Sleeve on an HT Lead

1. A plug or HT lead which won't transmit a spark when others are O.K. is difficult to prove faulty except by substitution. Visible chaffing or a split in a sleeve holding the

lead to the distributor, needs to be bound up – see fig. 37. But first you need to be sure a) that the metal connectors at each end of the lead securely penetrate a carbon filling or are soundly attached to a wire-strand core and b) that the metal end is firmly located in electrical contact at its attachment to the distributor. Figs. 23, page 62, and 36 and 37 show how to ensure these end connections are being made positively. With a suspect end-contact on a carbon filled lead you can cut off 1cm and screw the contact in afresh; it's worth a try but a generally broken down carbon filling requires replacement with new HT lead.

2. With *all* plug *leads* producing good sparks (read above if not) we can focus on the sparking plugs themselves. The attachment cap or fitting of the plug lead on to the plug must be sound, for which refer to 1) above, and the plug body – especially the ceramic part – must be clean and dry.

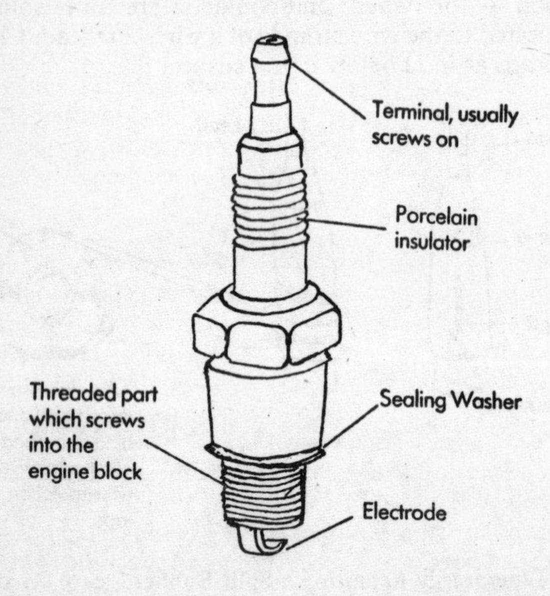

Fig. 38: Spark Plug
In older cars, sparking plug types are generally fatter-bodied and may have a shorter thread length; most also employ a sealing metal washer (as illustrated here).

Sparking splugs are subject to wear. The electrode (figs. 38/39) burns away, and good performance (not to mention fuel economy) is usually on the wane by 10,000 miles. The gap is best re-set at around 5,000 miles as a maintenance routine.

If you have a new set of exactly the right type handy and suspicion has centred on the plugs, the quickest thing to do is fit them. (If your plugs are old that is a worthwhile thing to do anyway.) If new ones (correctly gapped) don't solve your problem, double check the lead attachments as above and test the plugs as explained next, in case a new one is faulty. If that doesn't work see 5B/5 below.

Otherwise test the present plugs, and clean them up and re-set the gaps as below, or fit old but still working plugs (of the exact correct sort), again, correctly gapped, in order hopefully to solve your problem on a temporary basis.

To test, clean and reset the gaps of sparking plugs

So that the engine can turn with least effort it is sensible to remove all the plugs at once. First mark each HT lead and its corresponding plug *hole* in the engine block with chalk or a scratchmark so they can be re-matched in the proper firing order without difficulty, even if replacement plugs are eventually fitted.

Remove the HT leads and unscrew the plugs anti-clockwise. Take care not to crack the porcelain/ceramic upper body of the plug – the slightest careless jar with the plug spanner and they are usually gone! Reattach the HT leads to the plugs having an eye that the electrical connection is sound, as already emphasised. (* NOTE: If the electrodes of *all* your plugs come out *soaked* wet with petrol, have you been flooding the engine? See page 47.)

Test one plug at a time, folding the others to a safe position out of your way as you do each one. Watch that porcelain! Make sure they cannot fall. The plug being tested *must* have the threaded portion (fig. 38) resting on (touching firmly) the engine block, since that is the route via which the HT circuit returns to earth. Sellotape or insulating tape may be helpful to hold it there.

Turn the engine with the starter – *clothes, hands etc. clear of moving parts* – and look for a spark at the electrodes.

Alternatively the engine can be turned by hand via the drive belt. See page 70; remember ignition *on*.

Judging your spark
For each complete turn of the engine one good quality white/blue spark should spit across the electrodes' gap. You may need to shade the plug to see it.

A feeble orangy spark is most often a sign of a tired plug. Any sign of additional sparking up inside the plug body is a sign of age or dirt. In emergency, such a plug should be cleaned out as far as possible with an old toothbrush or similar item, and re-gapped (see fig. 39 and below). Much better is to replace it with a new or known-to-be-good plug.

A weak spark in a *good* plug would suggest problems further back in the HT or LT circuits, or a flattish battery – for which the sequential checks earlier in the rest of this chapter are appropriate.

Re-gapping a spark plug
Almost all engines require a .025"/.65mm plugs' gap but check your owner's instruction handbook. In the absence of feeler gauge and/or handbook, the thickness of a cardphone card provides an emergency measure. (Bank or credit cards are usually a fraction thicker.)

Never put a new or old plug in without setting the gap.

Fig. 39 shows how to set the gap. Only the top electrode is adjustable. As it usually needs closing toward the bottom one, and widening it is difficult without the special tool shown, a tip is to insert the feeler gauge before tapping it down so it can't go too far. If you don't have a hammer etc., tap the electrode on to a stone or pavement. Should you have to widen it again take care not to lever against the bottom electrode, which can be cracked easily.

Returning the plugs to the engine
A little engine oil off the dipstick (fig. 14, page 32) smeared round the threads inside the plughole may help if a plug is stiff to turn. A plug must be tightened right down to make a gas-tight seal, or engine compression will suffer – in which case fuel cannot burn, nor can the engine start. However it is

important not to overtighten the plugs which will result in damage too. They should be tightened until you feel real resistance and then given an extra quarter of a turn. The washer, which completes the gas-tight joint on the types which have a washer, should be squeezed – not obliterated!

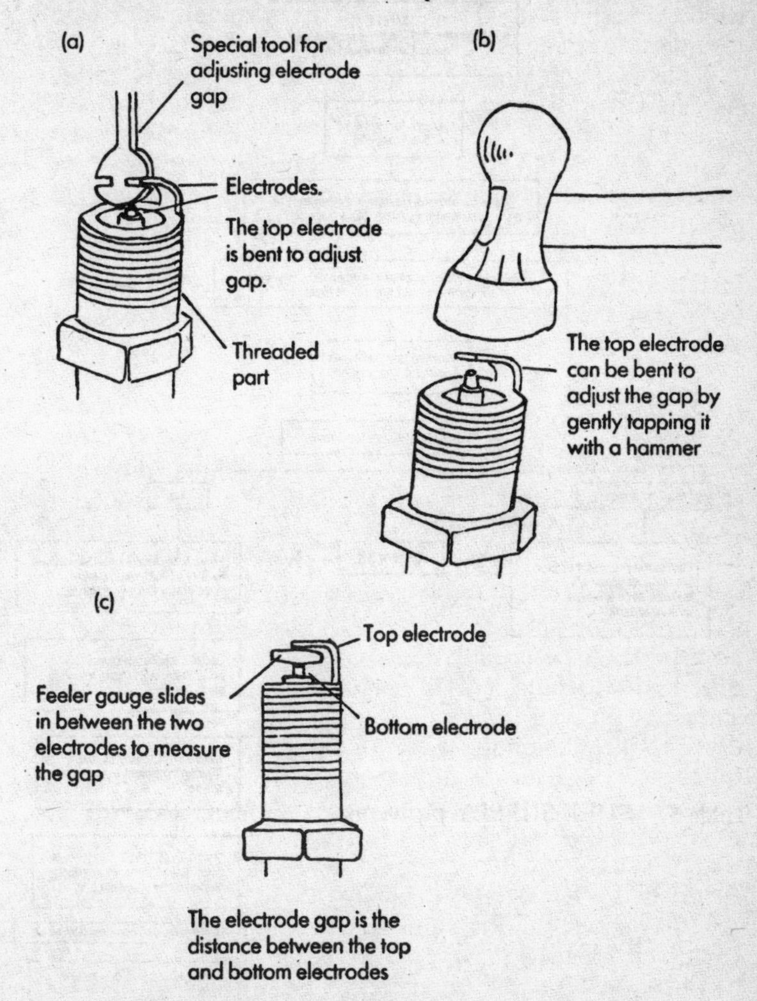

Fig 39: Adjusting the Electrode Gap on a Spark Plug
The feeler gauge should be a gripped but sliding fit.

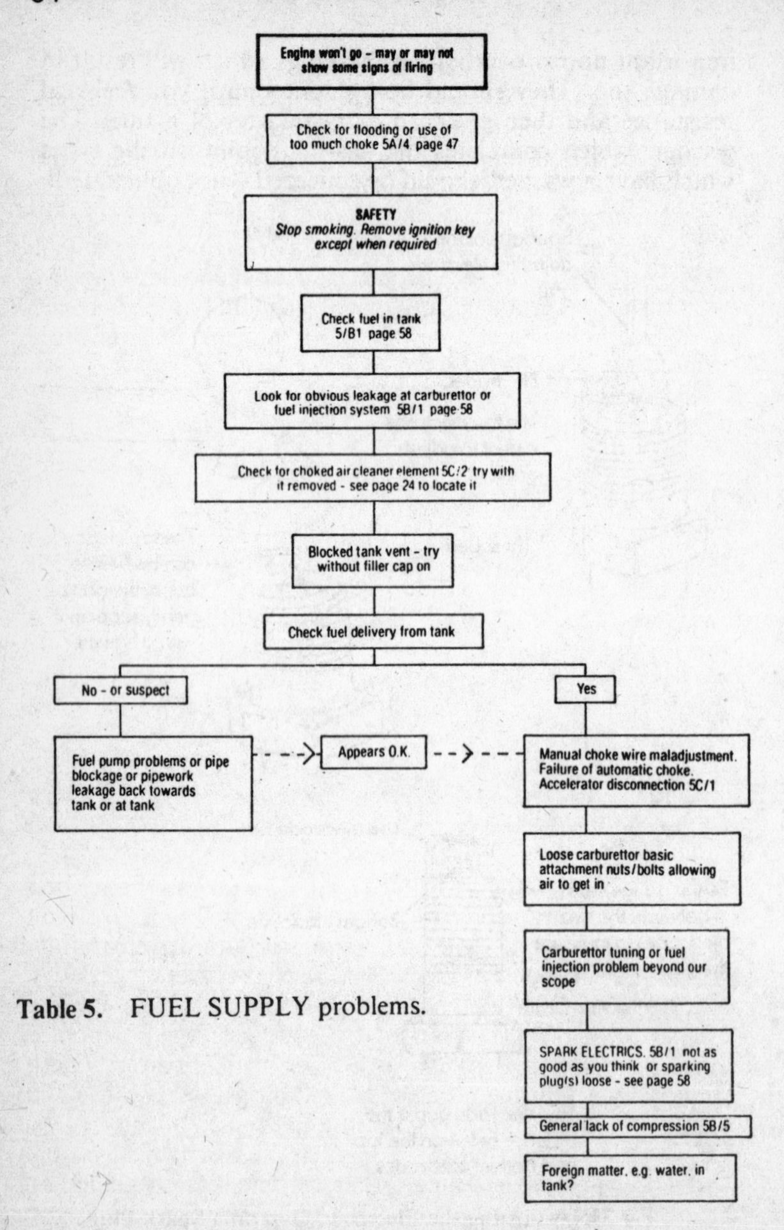

Table 5. FUEL SUPPLY problems.

5B/5 *Spark Electrics Fault Tracking*
Carrying out the NO and/or YES series of tests from Table 4, page 57, as expanded upon in this chapter thus far will, apart from freak faults, make sure you get good sparks at all your plugs.

If the *engine* still *won't go* it is possible the spark timing has been lost, or a major fault such as loss of engine compression has occurred. However, such things are beyond the scope of a roadside emergency book, except to say that an engine with weak compression may respond to a tow start just one more time, so refer to page 90.

Before you despair though – it is more likely to be trouble in the Fuel Supply, so move on with 5/C below.

5C/1 FUEL SUPPLY
If the engine turns over energetically and fires a bit but will not keep going, as mentioned on page 58, and particularly if you have found that all the spark plugs are sound, working well, and fitted tightly, then you have most probably got a *Fuel Supply* problem.

Table 5 maps the priorities for finding a fuel supply fault. Most will emerge via references elsewhere before the table divides to YES and NO at the fuel delivery check.

If the engine will start without the air cleaner element, put it back once the engine is running, having turned it round to a different position inside if that is possible . (See 5C/2). Get a new air filter element as soon as you can. If the engine turns out to run when the petrol filler cap is removed, the venting system within the cap has probably become blocked. If you can't find that blockage you may be able to drive carefully onwards with a temporary cap made on the lines suggested in fig. 48, page 115, fitted over the hole instead. Warning! The substitute cap must be secure; depending on the position of the filler opening petrol may otherwise swill out directly onto a back wheel during cornering, becoming a likely cause of a dangerous skid – not to mention a fire risk.

The fuel delivery check is only for the mechanically more adventurous. Nevertheless other readers, please glance on through Table 5 and below. There may be some things you can still do.

To establish whether fuel is reaching the carburettor or fuel injection system satisfactorily, you need to find the pipework union immediately adjacent to whichever you have – which arrives there from the fuel pump/tank. Undo the union carefully, being sure to retrieve a filter gauze if one is housed inside.

YOU ARE WARNED AGAIN: Petrol and its vapour is very dangerous. DO NOT SMOKE. Isolate the area around the undone union from the distributor and spark plugs, separating them with plastic sheeting or similar material. You will probably now need an assistant to hold a large absorbent rag over the end of the undone pipe to catch the fuel.

Switch on the ignition (*but not the starter*) for just 2 or 3 seconds, and switch off again. If your car has an electric fuel pump, petrol should have spurted vigorously from the end of the pipe.

If your car has a mechanical fuel pump driven by the engine you may have already recognised it as a dome-shaped appendage attached to the engine and linked to the petrol pipe within sight of where you have undone the union. Some of these have an obvious priming lever on the side which can be used to see if the pump works. If there is no priming lever you need to use the starter. The starter must turn for the absolute minimum time, which means switching it off almost as fast as you can react to realising it has begun to turn the engine. Again, the delivery of strong spurts of petrol will clear the pump from further suspicion. If all is O.K. the union should be done up again so as to be locked tight, but not so tight as to risk cracking the pipework or union assembly. Always check visually afterwards, when the engine is running again, that there is no leak.

We deal first with the NO side of Table 5. With an electric pump that is not working you may be able to find where it is (it can be anywhere along the pipework back to the tank – favourite places are: mounted at the side of the engine compartment, and inside the back wing near the tank, usually accessed via the boot) and give it a gentle thump or two which can provide a temporary repair! Check that the electrical connection is clean and tight. If you suspect an earthing fault, try a temporary flex – see 13C, page 137. Check the fuse – see Chapter 12A, page 131.

A blockage in the pipework may have happened. If you have strong lungs and don't mind the taste of petrol, try blowing down the pipe where you have undone it at the union back to the petrol tank. This may bring temporary relief. However, the blockage is likely to recur soon, necessitating a thorough clean-out of the fuel system.

Leakage in the pipework back towards the tank (either side of the pump) would prevent the pump pumping properly but you would be very lucky to find it, and cracked piping cannot be satisfactorily taped up.

Where you have evidence of a blockage, further roadside work may be worthwhile if you are mechanically inclined. The filter gauze at the fuel pump can be examined but I suggest you only have a go if you are good at fitting back together in the right order, things you take apart! On electric pumps the gauze is usually located at the inlet union; on mechanical pumps it is normally under the dome cover. All washers, gaskets (shaped material squeezed between joints) etc. must be restored undamaged to their rightful place. If the pipe from the tank can be undone at the pump, blowing back down it may release any blockage there.

That is about all you can do at the roadside if no fuel is being delivered from a tank known to have petrol in it.

Remember to do up all pipe unions etc. *now*, even if your problem has not been solved.

Cleaning out the fuel system/overhauling the pump which is the next stage, can be regarded as strictly a garage job, mainly for fire safety reasons. If you have released a blockage by blowing back, or discovering a badly choked, silted-up gauze, a thorough clean-out will almost certainly have to be done soon to avoid a repetition of your problems but at least you may be able to drive cautiously home.

Going on to the YES side of Table 5, watch the choke and accelerator linkages at the carburettor/fuel injection end, whilst an assistant works them from inside the car. A makeshift reconnection of the accelerator is not a very safe plan but there may be something obvious which you can fix with certainty, and thoroughly test before driving, *carefully* to the next garage. A choke linkage may just have come loose or the choke butterfly valve in the carburettor may not be able to maximise its opening/closing because of a stretched wire etc. This valve can usually be seen when the air cleaner is removed. You may be able to make the needed linkage adjustment, or to work the choke directly to get the engine started – setting it (tying it if need be) in the off position once the engine is warmed up. You may be able to hand operate an automatic choke and/or at least establish if that is your problem.

Carburettors/fuel injectors rarely go off tune sufficiently to prevent starting unless interfered with by amateurs, so this book leaves them to the experts. You are referred elsewhere via table 5, regarding Spark Electrics and possible compression faults.

Water-contaminated petrol caused by moisture condensing in the tank, especially in winter, can also be a problem. Its effect can be minimised by keeping a full tank of petrol as a general rule – should your car be sensitive to this problem.

Vandals getting at your petrol tank is a regrettable possibility which can only be dealt with by a clean-out at a garage aware of the fire safety risks.

5C/2 *Choked Air Filter*

An air filter functionally becomes gradually clogged with dirt. It is usual to replace the element at 10 to 12,000 miles before the choking effect begins to raise fuel consumption to any marked degree. A simple butterfly screw is normally all that has to be undone to get at the element, which consists of special fluted absorbent card held between 2 plastic ends. The card will probably be discoloured but the gaps between folds should not be clogged with dirt. If they are, try banging the filter gently on the ground or brushing it gently with an old toothbrush or similarly blunt instrument.

When you put it back, align the least dirty area with the air entry point if you can. Replace a choked filter with a new one as soon as practical.

6

JUMP-AND-BUMP STARTING

WHAT TO DO WHEN THE BATTERY IS FLAT OR THE STARTER FAILS

If you know why your battery is flat or nearly so, you may have turned direct to this chapter. Or maybe you hope to defer fuller investigations. Either way, attempting this sort of start may seem preferable to "getting your hands dirty" if you can avoid it.

Understood! But please appreciate a) pushers get tired! b) jump-leads take time to organise! and c) that although one of these methods will almost certainly work even when a battery is utterly dead (providing that is the ONLY problem), most Fuel Supply faults – apart from flooding or a dirty air cleaner, and most Spark Electric problems – other than mildly overdue replacement/cleaning of sparking plugs and contact breaker points, will PREVENT a jump-or-bump start working anyway.

Therefore unless you are pretty certain what is wrong and that it can be resolved later, you will save time if you go to Chapter 5 first. You won't need to read it all. It fast-tracks you wherever you can skip direct to a source of trouble. Looking there should reveal *why* your battery is in trouble. Having sorted that out, your assistants on a jump-or-bump start ought not to be wasting their time.

Ultimately the reason you needed a jump-or-bump start (e.g. a charging system fault, chapter 8B) always has to be found if you are to avoid repetitions.

* A bump (push or tow) start is generally not possible with automatic transmission. There are a few exceptions, e.g. certain cars which have an automatic drive on which you can "hold" in all 4 gears. The lever can be shifted into 2nd gear once the car is on the move in order to do the trick. The maker's instruction handbook will give details.

* If you have power steering or servo-brakes remind the driver that unless/until the engine runs, heavy hands and foot will be needed to work them.
* If the start is being attempted via a tow, refer to Chapter 10, about safety, signal for stopping etc.
* The driver must consider whether the engine has been flooded. If so, he may need to floor the accelerator initially as explained on page 47, 2). To turn the engine the equivalent of several more bursts will be easiest in top gear.
* Observe normal road safety. Driver(s) (both, for a tow start) is/are responsible. *See chapter 10.*

6A 'BUMP', PUSH OR TOW START

1. With the ignition turned *on*, (note that this releases the steering lock too) place the car in third or fourth gear with the clutch pedal *depressed* and the handbrake *off*, but with your other foot on the footbrake. For a cold start a manual choke should be out as normal, but see **2**, page 47.

2. At a pre-arranged signal the push or tow can begin. See chapter 10 first if you are doing a tow start.

3. Once the car is moving at a fast walking pace, you briskly engage the gear by letting up the clutch pedal fully and simultaneously relating the accelerator position to this speed. The engine should burst into life within a few revolutions.

4. The push/tow needs to *continue* until the engine begins to pull the car. A manual choke may need pushing back in temporarily to prevent flooding. Once it is definitely pulling, even if a touch jerkily, you can put the clutch pedal down and encourage the engine with the accelerator. Signal to a tow-er (by the sign previously agreed) to stop *gently* whilst you pull up using the handbrake. (You will find that pushers have given up already, so a handbrake stop won't bother them!)

5. Keep the engine revving well, until it will idle by itself.

6. Even if the engine does not start the first time you try, try again, especially if the engine makes "encouraging" sounds.

7. A flooded engine will need a good 25 metres turning over in top gear with the accelerator floored to hope to clear it. Equally a flat battery needs a long distance push. However, with several pushers it is not too difficult in top gear. With a tow, there is obviously more scope.

6B JUMP-LEAD STARTING

Given a "slave" car and a good pair of jump-leads (see page 14) this is usually far easier than pushing or towing. With the slave car's engine running you can give reasonably long bursts on your starter without fear of flattening the slave battery. This helps if you think your engine is flooded and needs clearing.

* DO – follow the HOT or COLD starting notes on pages 46/7/8.
* Remember road safety *first*, before bringing the slave car alongside.
* If your car (unusually) has a positive earth, that is with the red (+) battery terminal connected to the body and/or engine, instead of the black (–) terminal, you still connect the red (+) terminal to red (+), and the black (–) to black (–). The only difference is that in that case the black lead will be the live output one to be especially careful with (see below).

* Warning! The electrolyte in a flat battery is more prone to freezing in arctic weather. *It must be thawed out* before jump leads are used.

1. Bring the slave car in on yours, having established the best way to have the 2 batteries nearest each other. The 2 batteries must be of the same voltage, e.g. 12 volt to 12 volt. The cars must not touch.
2. Switch *off* the ignition in both cars.
3. Connect the red jump-lead between the (+) or output terminals on the two batteries. Establish for certain before you begin, which ones they are (see above *). The instant you have fixed one end, the lead becomes LIVE! Don't wave it about or touch anything except the correct terminal on the other battery. (A mistake might damage an alternator.) Make sure that good contacts are made – they should not for example, come apart simply by touching them with the hand.
4. Connect the black jump-lead to the (–) or earth return terminal of both batteries, with the same care. An alternative and possibly safer method is to connect the negative lead from the boost battery to the engine block or a major body earth point on the car with the flat battery.

WARNING: Always deal with each lead separately. If you attach both to one battery first you are almost bound to touch the ends together and could easily burn yourself with the short-circuit caused.

5. Start the car with the *good* battery and have someone hold the accelerator STEADY at a fast tick-over. The engine *must not be raced at any time*.
6. You can now start your engine in the normal way but you also must keep the revs low – whatever you do, *do not race the engine*.
7. *Wait* till your engine will run quietly without stalling before:
8. Removing the jump-leads carefully, *one* complete lead at a time. As in connecting up – do not wave the end of a live lead around!

To avoid damage to either cars' alternator it is essential that both engines are running quietly, at the moment of disconnection.

Note that the battery in a car must NEVER be disconnected except when the engine is stopped for the same reason.

7

ENGINE OVERHEATING

WARNINGS: First, electric fans can be dangerous, suddenly coming on long after the engine and ignition are off. Find out if yours is electric – see Chapter 4, page 31 for identification, and Section 7C/1 below on Safety. Second, OUCH! Touch *nothing* till it has cooled down. See Safety "do's and don'ts" numbers 7–9, page 12 and relevant text here.

As Chapter 8 makes clear it is a foolish driver indeed who ignores a temperature gauge or warning light signalling overheating, an oil pressure warning lamp, or a charging system light alerting to a possible broken drive belt.

Stop at once and investigate.

Similarly, if you suddenly start losing power, stop and look. You could have partial piston seizure *and* overheating. Partial seizure normally disappears with cooling down. Provided further overheating is prevented, little damage should be caused. Longer term power loss usually involves other factors, or ones outside our scope here but see 7K below (perhaps you have forgotten to let off your handbrake . . .).

If your nostrils detect any hot smell, stop and find out where it is coming from. By the time you see steam billowing out you may be in real trouble . . .

An overheated engine – even for a very few miles – can be the most expensive emergency your engine may suffer. Never assume that you can go on slowly home. It could be the worst mistake you ever made. Once heat has distorted the cylinder head or something has seized solid, bills can run into 100s of £££s, or even 1,000s of £££s if a new engine has to be fitted. And it can all happen in moments if the driver just does not realise that the fan drive-belt has broken, or whatever. Chapter 8 on the significance of dashboard idiot lights repays careful study.

What to do

1. Pull off the road and open the bonnet *carefully* as there may be scalding steam about.
2. Switch the interior heater to Hot and run the de-mister full-speed to help cool the engine. Touch nothing until the engine is properly cooled down. Wait at least 30 to 35 minutes.
3. You can be looking for more obvious trouble spots while you wait *but keep your hands off and your face well clear*: is steam or water coming from anywhere on the radiator – especially around the cap, or from any of the rubber pipes that may be carrying the water supply around the engine? If you can see the source you can start thinking how to get it mended. Meanwhile refer to Table 6.

Once the engine has cooled considerably you can help speed up the process of removing – with care as follows – the radiator cap, if one is fitted. Press it down and turn it in an anti-clockwise direction. It is best if the whole cap is covered with a cloth and then turned *very slowly*, a mere fraction to start with. Provided you have waited long enough, this should allow any further steam to escape gradually and avoid any eruption of boiling water. Once the pressure has dissipated the cap can be cautiously removed. Great care is needed to avoid scalding! Do *not* have your face directly over the cap!

Older cars tend to have spring-loaded radiator caps that simply allowed overheated coolant to expand and flow out. Most cars now have an ordinary radiator cap and an expansion bottle system as explained in Chapter 4, page 28 and figs. 10 and 11. Posh cars have no radiator cap and employ a Header Expansion tank. Check the system your car has and make sure you open the expansion bottle as well as the radiator cap if applicable, or just the expansion tank where no radiator cap is provided.

A puzzling form of overheating afflicts just a very few cars. The unusual feature is that it only happens *after* switching off, and generally only in very hot climatic conditions after a long fast run. The remedy is to start the engine and let it tick-over for a while before switching off again. This allows the coolant to circulate more effectively around parts which normally rely partly on air flow during high speed driving.

* No physical signs — yet!	* Temperature gauge at red/danger or temp. warning light on (or charge system light on above idling speed, or oil pressure warning lamp on when engine running)

* Investigate at once.

Causes in the table below are given in the best sequential order for investigation; so unless the cause is clear (e.g. severe neglect to check your oil or coolant levels), work through them in order.

Coolant steaming, spurting, leaking from:	Possible cause of overheating:
Radiator cap or expansion chamber, or nowhere as yet	Coolant level (7A) Air flow across radiator blocked (7B) Malfunctioning fan (7C) Leaking radiator cap (7D) Dud thermostat (7E) Oil loss, or level too low (7F) Frozen coolant (7G – arctic weather only) Water pump failure (7H)
Rubber pipes (known as radiator hoses)	Split pipe, or poor connections (7I)
Radiator elsewhere	Cracked radiator (7J)
Overheating Factors beyond scope of book (7K)	

Table 6. Engine Overheating.

7A *Coolant level*
This section assumes you have taken care to allow the engine to cool as warned above.

1. If the coolant level is too low (even by a kettleful), then the engine will overheat. The coolant level should be about an inch below the level of a radiator cap, and above any structures you can see inside. Where there is an expansion bottle or header tank, coolant is topped up via that and the level should be visible between the "Maximum" and "Minimum" marks on the side of it. See fig. 10, page 28.

Coolant level should be routinely checked – see Chapter 17.

A coolant shortage *itself*, may have caused your overheating but that is unlikely unless it has "never" been checked. BEFORE DRIVING ON you must establish and eliminate the cause. If you are not on to the culprit already, carry on below till you find it.

Having cured it you MUST remember to top up the coolant and replace the radiator cap and/or expansion chamber top "afore ye go". And, then watch your temperature gauge to be sure it settles in the normal happy position!

2. *Coolant* means a mixture of water and anti-freeze, although water alone will suffice in an emergency. Remember in that case that the anti-freeze component will need adjustment as soon as possible since it affects the boiling point of the coolant. Water must be clean. If you have to take some from a stream strain it through a handkerchief.

> WARNING: *Do not* attempt to re-fill a hot engine radiator with cold water. This could result in a cracked engine or cylinder head block. Wait at least half an hour while things cool off; then do it *slowly*, adding a small amount of water at a time and giving it the chance to warm up before adding more.

If you have to replace more than say half a bucketful of coolant, air may be trapped inside the system. It cannot function 100% effectively until such air is driven out. Ridding the system properly of air is a garage job on more complicated engines. But for straightforward ones and for emergency purposes the thing to do is to check the re-filling several times before the engine is fully hot, and at least once after that – which will mean a further 30–35 minute stop while it cools (see page 94) – so as to top up again if need be, until the system settles down and you are confident it is remaining full, i.e. has had the air driven out and/or is no longer leaking. Whatever you do, don't let the engine overheat again! For full anti-frost protection owners are encouraged to change the entire coolant at least every 2 years. It loses its anti-frost strength over time.

7B *Radiator air flow*
Examine the radiator fins (see fig. 10, page 28). If there is excessive dirt blocking a high proportion of the space between the fins, or a sheet of paper or anything that would prevent the flow of air, stuck to the radiator, the offender must be removed. Any severe blockage is probably the cause of overheating. A high pressure hose is best for ridding the fins of mud etc. but cover the ignition electrics from getting wet.

7C *Malfunctioning fan*
If the fan fails to work properly, insufficient air will be drawn over the radiator. This is especially critical in slow-moving traffic.

You may have a loose or broken drive belt affecting both a continuously driven fan and the water pump, or you may just have a faulty electric fan. Notice that you could have a sound electric fan but a slack or broken drive belt preventing proper water circulation and thus causing some overheating. To check and adjust a suspiciously loose belt see 7C/3, page 101.

7C/1 *Electric fan*
An electric fan (fig. 13, page 31) is controlled by a thermoswitch so that it only comes on when the temperature rises to a predetermined safe level, and it goes off again when the temperature falls. Most drivers are familiar with the noise these fans make during engine idling, so absence of noise ought to be noted quite quickly.

Just because this type of fan does not operate all the time, do *not* assume when you stop your car and switch off the ignition that it is safe to touch the blades. When you stop a hot engine it goes on getting hotter (because the oil and coolant stop being circulated) before it starts to cool off. Most cars are therefore wired so that the fan *will* continue to operate periodically as required until the engine has genuinely started to cool off. The safest policy is never to touch the fan blades; there is no reason why you should anyway.

When this type of fan fails to come on before the engine overheats, check that the electrical connections to the electric motor and to the thermoswitch are clean and tight. The thermoswitch is mounted directly into the radiator as in fig. 13. It usually has 2 push-on electrical connections of the spade type depicted in fig. 26, page 66.

If you remove these 2 wire connectors and touch them together temporarily the fan should spring into life, even (usually but not always) with the ignition *off*. If it does you have probably alighted on the trouble spot. In an emergency you may be able to make some progress homeward/garage-ward by joining the wires more permanently so that the fan can run all the time during urban traffic conditions; but you will have to separate them to stop the fan on the open road in order to avoid *over-cooling* which is not good for the engine either. The hopping in and out to deal with the wires may be a bit tedious and you will have to keep a hawk-eye on your temperature gauge or warning light but at least this provides a get-you-home possibility. However, neither author nor publisher can accept responsibility for any consequences should you not notice overheating or over-cooling in an attempt to drive on.

If touching the wires does not bring on the fan, the electric motor itself, or its connection, are at fault, or a fuse has blown. Check especially where the 2nd wire to the motor – not the one from the thermoswitch – is earthed. The attachment there must be clean bright metal-to-metal. If you have a length of flex handy (Chapter 2, page 15) you could temporarily bypass the input wiring (including the thermo-switch) by running it from the battery output direct to the input contact on the motor. If that works you have a wiring problem somewhere but you might be able to drive on on the emergency basis just described. You would have to try it if a spare fuse blew again immediately. To check for a blown fuse refer to your car maker's operating instructions handbook.

Other than above, a failed electric fan is a garage job. Note that it is possible for a faulty thermoswitch merely to stray above its pre-set switching temperature so that the fan comes in too late and goes off again too early. Once more it is a new switch you need although you might finish your present journey on the lines described already.

Remember your troubles may not be at the fan alone. See 7C/2 below and check that your drive belt is in good order.

7C/2 *Continuously driven fan*

The most common cause of a malfunctioning fan is a loose or broken drive belt. Fig. 12 and pages 30/31 describe the normal arrangements.

If a fan drive belt snaps, both the water pump and the fan stop. Rapid overheating results. A slack belt reduces the efficiency of the water pump and fan and would cause partial overheating. Adjusting a loose belt to take up the slackness is described in 7C/3 below. First let's look at a broken fan belt emergency. They are not repairable so an alternative must be found:

1. The commercially available emergency fan belts are best (unless you have a proper replacement, the time to fit it – and you do not mind getting yourself a bit mucky, in which case see 7C/3 below). The emergency belts fit any make of car without having to undo anything, and come with full instructions.
2. You can makeshift with a suitable thin rope or a pair of tights, to get the car to the nearest garage. Tights/rope are fitted around the 3 pulleys – twice round if possible for greater friction – as tight as you can and then knotted. The loose ends must be cut off as in fig. 40(a) so that they cannot get caught in any moving parts. If the arrangement slips immediately when you try starting the engine you will have to get the makeshift belt tighter. The best way is to slacken off the alternator/dynamo bolts as described in 7C/3 and adjust its position to get the tension good.
3. If adjusting the tension is beyond your immediate scope or you only have short tights . . . you could makeshift around

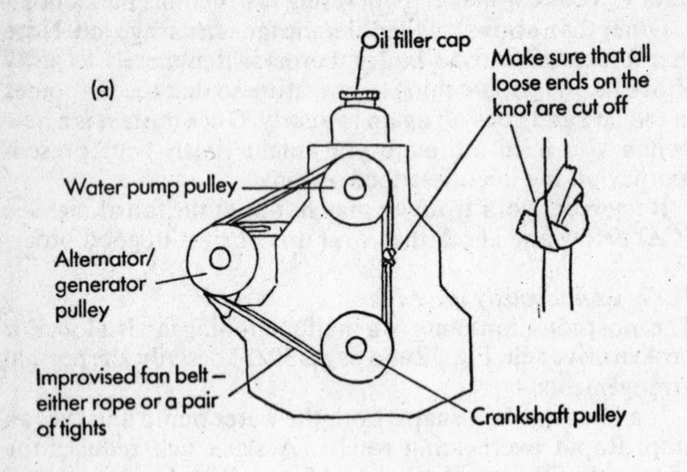

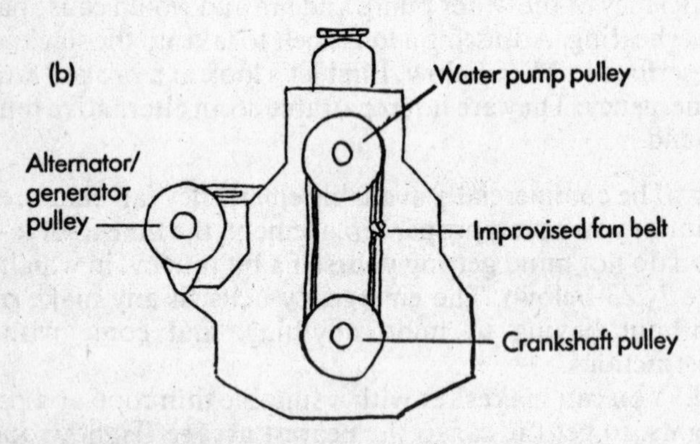

Fig. 40: Improvising a Fan-Belt in an Emergency
(a) Using the Three Pulleys
(b) Using Only Two Pulleys

only 2 of the pulleys, the crankshaft and the water pump as in fig. 40(b). As the alternator/dynamo will then be out of action, only try this if your battery is O.K., if it is daylight and you are not far from a garage. Conserve electricity by having all possible electrics off as you drive to get further help.

7C/3 Fitting a replacement fan drive belt/tightening a slack belt

Fan belt tightness is adjusted by altering the position of the alternator/dynamo pulley. The other 2 pulleys are in fixed positions.

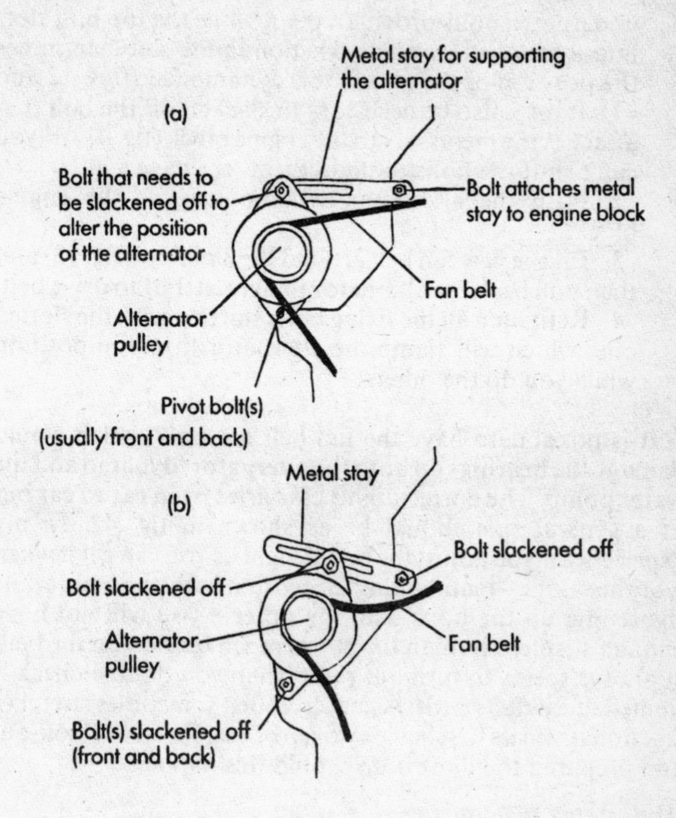

Fig. 41: Adjusting the Tension of the Fan-Belt by Varying the Position of the Alternator/Dynamo

The device may pivot on 2 bolts – front and back – or one "through" bolt as in fig. 12, page 30.

(a) Alternator Position with Fan-Belt Tight

(b) Alternator Position with Fan-Belt Loose

A dynamo position is adjusted in exactly the same way.

1. Slacken off all the alternator/dynamo mounting bolt(s). *Do not undo them completely.* They slacken anti-clockwise; hold the nut and turn the bolthead or vice versa. Simply turn the bolthead if it is directly screwed into the engine block. There are either 2 or 3 fixing points – usually 1 on top, and either 1 or 2 underneath. The underneath bolts provide a pivot while the top bolt slots into a metal stay and its position in the slot determines the position of the alternator/dynamo (see figs. 12 and 41). It may also be necessary to slacken off the bolt that attaches the metal stay to the engine block (fig. 41). If you can't shift the bolts to undo them, see page 150.
2. Push the alternator/dynamo *towards* the engine block.
3. Fit the new fan belt around the 3 pulleys (fig. 12) and then pull back the alternator to tighten the fan drive belt.
4. Retighten all the fixing bolts starting with the slotted one, which will clamp the alternator firmly in position while you do the others.

It is possible to have the fan belt *too tight* which would damage the bearings on both the alternator/dynamo and the water pump. The correct tightness varies from car to car but as a general rule should be as shown in fig. 42. In my experience if you adjust the belt as tight as you can get it when working alone – maintaining the tension with one hand while tightening up the bolts with the other – you will not have enough surplus strength to get too much tension on the belt. It always seems to turn out right when you double-check it immediately afterwards. A new drive belt sometimes stretches fractionally in its first half day or so of use. Be on the look-out and prepared to adjust it up should this happen.

7D *Leaking radiator cap*

Since the cooling system is pressurised, coolant may be blowing out of a defective cap. There is no real test to prove this except substitution with a new one. It is the type on older cars (page 94) that most often causes trouble, which is why carrying a spare was suggested in Chapter 2. WARNING: Unless the engine is stone-cold, removal of the cap can be dangerous – see page 94. The underside of the cap and the

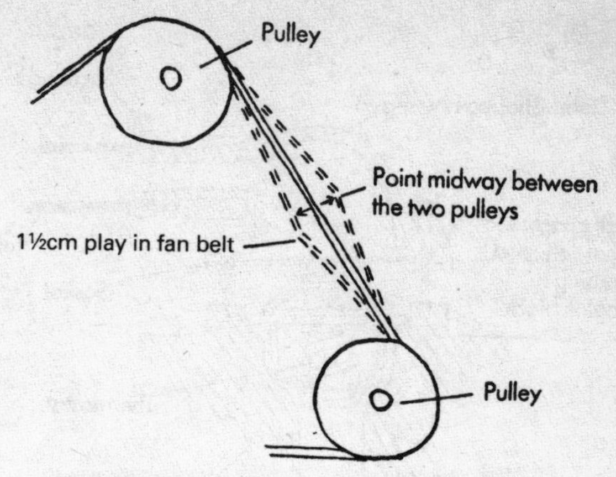

Fig. 42: Correct Tension of the Fan-Belt

rubber seal should be clean and in good condition. If you have to travel on with a duff cap, you will have a lot of stopping and waiting to cool down, and topping up to do. Whatever happens you must not allow the engine to overheat any more (see page 93).

7E *Dud thermostat*

The thermostat controls the flow of coolant through the engine block, being closed to prevent coolant flow when it is cold, and open, allowing coolant to flow when the engine is hot. A thermostat stuck open will result in the engine taking a long time to warm up and possibly in an inefficient heater. (The same happens if the thermostat is temporarily removed.) A thermostat stuck closed will cause overheating. A more detailed clue which may reveal a stuck-closed thermostat is a top hose which stays cooler to touch than the bottom hose or the engine itself. See fig. 11, page 29.

If you suspect a stuck-closed thermostat the best thing is to remove it. The engine will be perfectly able to function without a thermostat, although it is best to fit a new one as soon as possible because a slow warm-up causes undue extra wear and tear and wastes fuel.

The thermostat is usually located at the top radiator hose adjacent to where it joins the engine block. See Chapter 4, and fig. 11, and figs. 43 and 44.

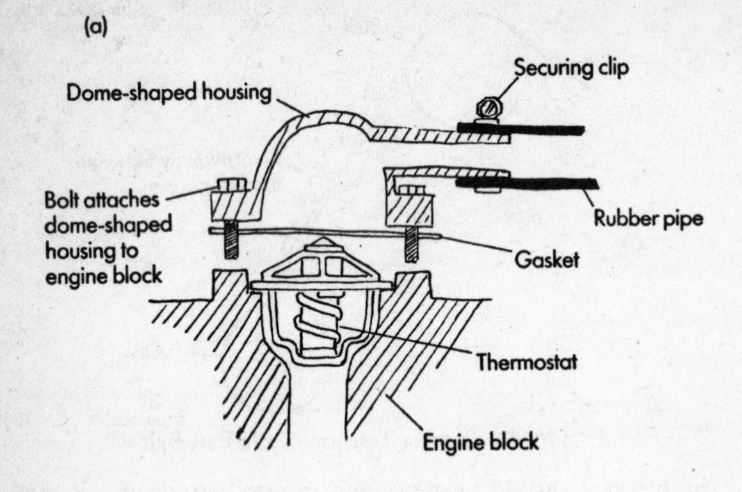

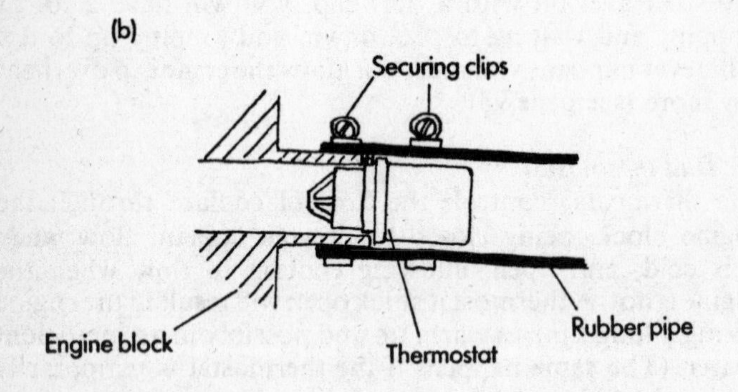

Fig. 43: Detailed Location of the Thermostat
(a) Thermostat Contained in Dome-shaped Housing
(b) Thermostat Contained Inside Rubber Pipe

To remove the thermostat

SAFETY: before undoing anything, think! Scalding hot coolant is likely to cascade out. Beware! The thermostat itself may still be too hot to handle.

How to get the thermostat out should be obvious once you look at figs. 43 and 44. If you have the type located under a domed housing, undo the nuts and carefully prize the housing

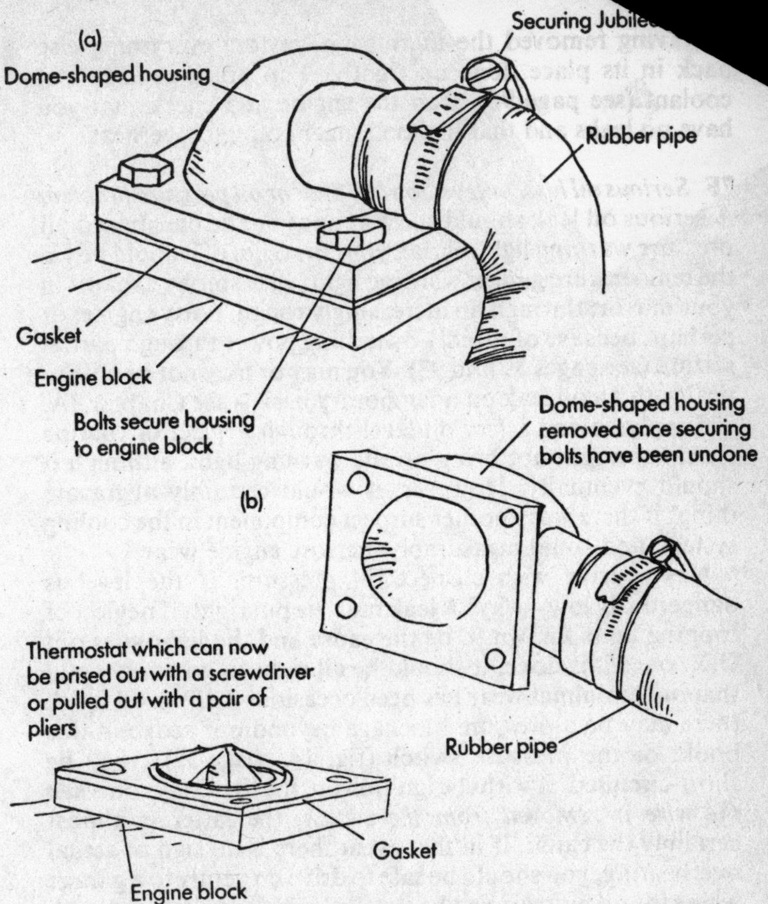

Fig. 44: Dome-shaped Structure Housing the Thermostat, and the Removal of the Thermostat
(a) External View
(b) Removal

away from the engine block. Between this housing and the block is a thin piece of shaped card (gasket) which is required for a completely sealed joint. It can be used again providing you do not badly damage it. If the gasket sticks to the top or bottom, ease it free with a penknife blade before lifting the dome right off. If it is damaged it must be replaced – see Chapter 16F for a temporary substitute.

, thermostat, restore everything else
ie up tightly. Top up to replace lost
6). Run the engine and check that you
that it is no longer going to overheat.

oss, or level too low and/ or oil pressure problem
A se... leak should show at once on the dashboard oil pressure ...rning light. If not, your first sign of it could be via the temperature gauge/warning light; via a smoky exhaust in your mirror; through an increasingly rough, noisy engine; or perhaps because of rapidly dwindling power through partial seizure (see pages 39 and 93). You may or may not be able to deal with an oil leak on a temporary basis – see Chapter 8A.

Simply having a low oil level through neglect of routine checking might not bring on the warning light, although it should eventually. However, it would certainly aggravate things if there was another suspect component in the cooling system, and could measurably increase engine wear.

Never drive with suspect oil pressure. If the level is dangerously low – why? A leak must be put right. If neglect of topping up is known to be the cause and the light goes out O.K. once it is done, it should be all right to go on, hopeful that only minimal wear has been occasioned. If the oil is full there may be a pressure blockage beyond our scope in this book, or the pressure switch (fig. 14, page 32) may be short-circuited. If with the ignition on, the light stays on *when the wire is removed from the switch*, the latter is almost certainly the cause. If in that event there is no sign of actual overheating, you should be safe to drive on gently to a garage where the oil pressure can be checked and the switch replaced.

7G *Frozen coolant*
Hopefully this can only occur if the anti-freeze constituent of the coolant is insufficient for arctic weather! The sign of it is when clouds of steam ensue well before the engine would normally have warmed up, allowing for the cold weather. Whilst some coolant boils the rest is blocked from circulating by the icing up. Waiting with your fingers crossed and the engine switched off, while the heat starting to build up in the engine seeps through the ice, trying again AT YOUR OWN

RISK *bit-by-bit*, once things are nearly stone cold again is about all you can do. The objective is for the defrosting to happen as slowly as possible.

If the water pump is frozen – unfortunately you cannot see if it is or not – then prematurely running the engine for too long risks destroying the water pump bearings, and increases the possibility of a fire. Be patient!

With luck the frozen part may only be the radiator which might survive providing the ice melts slowly. Otherwise you may find a cracked block or cylinder head either now, or when the snow melts . . . If apparently lucky with no leaks appearing anywhere once you have topped-up – SAFETY: see page 94 – make sure you get a garage to sort out the anti-freeze directly, or have the cooling system drained if you have to leave the car in the freeze-up.

7H *Water pump failure*

Apart from a mechanical fault within the pump but outside our scope, a loose or broken drive belt is the only cause. See 7C/3. If you are able to look inside the radiator whilst the engine warms up there should be signs of circulation once the thermostat opens but well before boiling point is reached.

7I *Perished rubber pipes and poor connections*

The rubber hoses of the cooling system are subject to perishing and splits – especially at their ends but sometimes along their length too. Once the engine has cooled off sufficiently (see page 94), if you are unsure exactly where water may be leaking (as so often), pipes can be examined by hand. Remember that water inside which may leak when you touch the pipe can still be very much hotter than the outside of the pipe, so be careful.

1. Feel along the pipes, bending them where possible as in fig. 45 to locate any leak.
2. A leak at an end joint end may be cured by simply tightening up the securing clip. But if there is a split as well or it still leaks, the pipe needs replacement, shortening (if possible – check the length first!), or temporary binding.

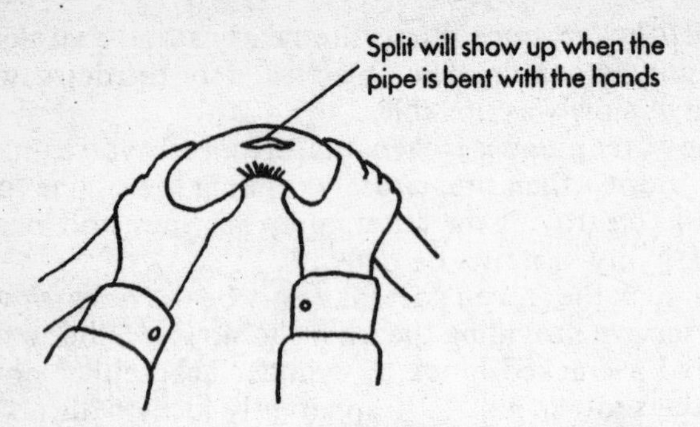

Fig. 45: Identification of Splits in the Rubber Pipes of the Cooling System

> WARNING: hot, possibly scalding, coolant will fountain out once a pipe comes free. How much, depends how high the remaining coolant level is compared with the pipe – i.e. a *lot* for a bottom hose! Be ready to get out of its way.

Undo the clips at both ends. Remove a pipe by pulling. If it has "bonded" itself to the metal stub the best way to break this bond is by twisting the pipe back and forth as if you were screwing/unscrewing it from the stub.

3. Unless you have a replacement pipe you need to dry the old one thoroughly before making an emergency repair. If you have a D.I.Y. hose repair kit as suggested in Chapter 2, follow the instructions with it. If not, try *plenty* of insulating tape (with the emphasis on plenty!). This will certainly be very temporary, so keep an eye on it, but it might last long enough to reach help.

If the leak is due to a split at one of the connections, get as much binding on it as will fit under the clip when you put that back.

4. *Jubilee Clips* (like bracelets, but tightenable by a screw) were recommended in Chapter 2. These will always do a better job than re-using original clips of any other type.

5. Remember to top up the cooling system before testing it and driving on. Watch your temperature gauge of course but don't leave it too long before having a 2nd, and later a 3rd

physical inspection of your handiwork in case it is not as good as you are hoping (see page 94 on Safety before checking hot system).

7J *Cracked radiator (leaking)*
Although ultimately this means professional repairs or a new radiator are needed, there is still something which can be done in an emergency if you have the necessary sealant recommended in Chapter 2. These sealants are quite effective and long-lasting for small leaks (which the majority are) in the radiator. Follow exactly the instructions thereon.

In the absence of one of these proprietary sealants a desperate measure which is known sometimes to work is the use of a hen egg. Once the engine has cooled down completely, crack a fresh egg into the radiator (throw the shell away). Run the engine gently for a few minutes so that the egg can circulate and plug the holes. Obviously the measure is extremely temporary and somewhat messy!

With either of the above 2 emergency possibilities you may be lucky enough to gain a repair which will last until you can get the car to a garage.

Be sure to top up the system before setting off, and to check frequently that you are not losing coolant again. Please be warned again about scalding coolant. If you have not yet read the rest of this chapter prior to this section please read it now, and take care of your safety. When proper repairs are done (as soon as possible) the whole system will have to be flushed out.

7K *Overheating due to maladjusted, binding brakes*
Do the wheels smell unusually hot? Have you driven miles with the handbrake on? If you have, there is a good chance that the heat created by friction will have caused problems with your brake hydraulic fluid. Refer to your maker's instruction handbook and check that there has been no loss of hydraulic fluid. If there has been no loss and the brakes work normally when you test them, you should be O.K. to drive on, but have the braking system inspected at the earliest opportunity. You cannot afford to take the risk that unseen damage might lead to faulty brakes within quite a short time–

before the next service inspection might reveal pending trouble.

If the brakes have been the cause of engine overheating, do not forget to check the coolant level as well, see 7A above.

7L *Overheating factors beyond the scope of this book*

An engine long due for overhaul may overheat as it becomes increasingly out of tune. The usual culprits in this case often cause reduced power as well. They are: much retarded ignition timing (sometimes this will be due to failure of the vacuum advance unit – see page 123); very weak fuel mixture; faulty (inlet/exhaust) combustion chamber valves, or the timing thereof.

However, you may just have a water blockage somewhere or a generally furred up system (like a furred kettle) – neither of which are easy to fix at the roadside. Motorists' D.I.Y. stores sell de-furring liquid preparations which you might try so long as you are prepared to find that the result of using them is lots of little leaks that had previously been plugged by the fur.

You may have a cylinder head gasket leak internally (or externally with a whistle!). Signs would be oil in the coolant, or a "magically" rising dipstick oil level as coolant finds its way there.

8

WHAT TO DO WHEN AN "IDIOT" LIGHT COMES ON

Oil Pressure – Charging System – Overheating – Brakes

Only 4 of the dashboard warning lights fall within our scope if they come on whilst the engine is running or you are driving along.

1. The oil pressure warning light (often has the symbol of an oil can) – see 8A.
2. The charging light (the symbol is often ϟ), see 8B.

   Lights 1. and 2. are ones that come on when the ignition switch is turned on and go out once the engine has started.
3. Temperature warning light – symbol is usually a thermometer – or there may be a gauge divided into "cold", "normal", "danger" (red sector) etc., see 8C.
4. If the brake warning light (drum brakes symbol) comes on, you should pull in and stop as soon as you can (this may require the handbrake). On some cars the light will come on when new brake pads are imminently required, and the owner's instruction handbook will advise you whether (if that is the case) it is safe to drive slowly to the nearest garage. *However, the light may have come on due to a dangerous degree of brake fluid loss*, so you must investigate properly what has happened. Again, the instruction handbook will advise you what course of action needs to be taken. This will probably depend on whether the brake fluid level is still, *and stays*, above the minimum in the reservoir or not.

8A *Oil pressure warning light comes on*
This warns that the oil pressure in the engine is dangerously outside its proper limits, and if ignored could lead to overheating, seizure of moving components and total ruin of the engine!

If the light comes on suddenly and stays ON:
1. Stop the car as *soon* as it is safe to do so. Check the dip-stick. (See fig. 14, page 32 if need.) You may need to roll/push the car safely on to level ground first; don't forget the ignition key needs to be turned on to free the steering lock, and that power steering and/or servo-brakes are much heavier to work when the engine is not running!

If the oil is *full* it is possible the warning light switch is faulty or the wiring has short circuited (see page 106) but more likely you have a serious oilway blockage somewhere, beyond the scope of this book and which means you must call professional help.
2. If the oil is low but not far below the MIN mark on the dip-stick it may just be failure to top up. A low oil level itself marginally increases usage as well as wear and tear on the engine. Few engines burn less than ½ litre in 1,000 miles. *However, it could also be a leak, so inspect fully as below.*

If the dip-stick shows well below the minimum oil left, examine underneath the car for signs of an oil leak. Figs. 2, 14 and 46 may help you. If the drain plug to the sump has come out, first take a long shot and look on the ground under the car in case it's there, in which case screw it back in and tighten it up. Otherwise use either a cork plug or a piece of wood whittled to the right shape with a penknife (fig. 46) or even another bolt wrapped with insulating tape (fig. 47). Such makeshift arrangements naturally must be checked frequently on the way to the nearest garage pending a proper replacement. See also 3, below.

If a leak is not at the drain plug or yet obvious, now check around the oil filter which is situated low down on the engine block (fig. 14 *and* page 33). Tighten it up if it appears to be leaking. They are mostly designed to be tightened sufficiently, simply by hand but you will have to wipe clean any excess oil to prevent your hands slipping. A clean, dry rag around the filter can be an extra help in getting it tight. You may need to

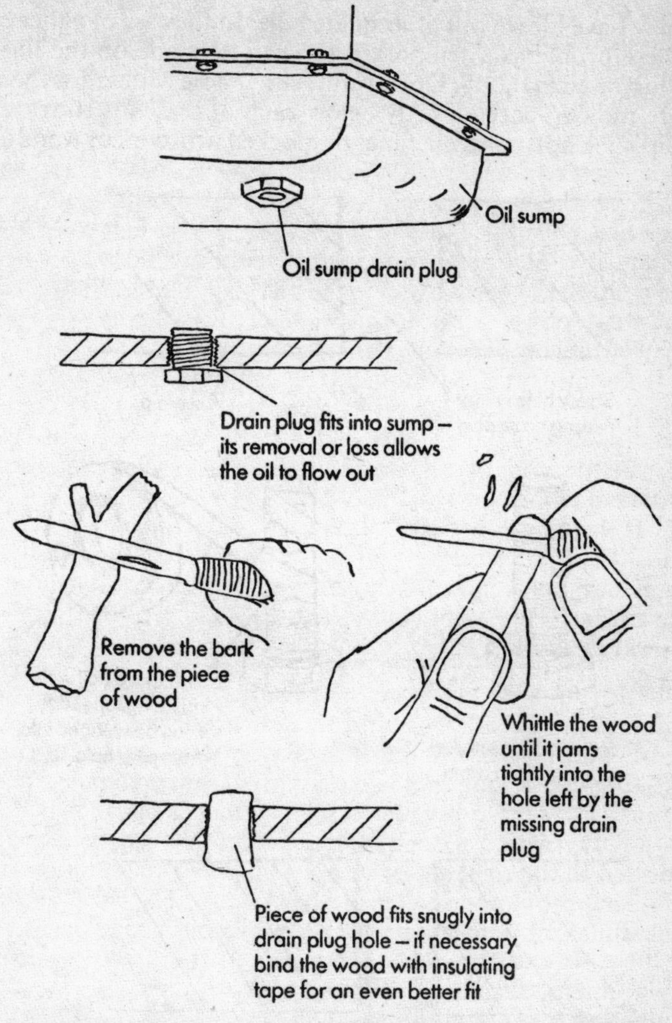

Fig. 46: Plugging of a Leaking Oil Sump with a Piece of Wood

make up a temporary gasket – see page 152 – if a normal one is torn.

Sometimes oil is lost upwards! Look at the underside of the bonnet. If the oil filler cap has come off you may have oil almost everywhere. If the dip-stick has gone missing some oil may have blown out of its guide hole. In the case of either of these problems a temporary top can be made on the lines illustrated in fig. 48. Do not stuff either hole with rag as there are moving parts directly below each of these apertures. A dip-stick hole can sometimes be blocked with cork or wood as

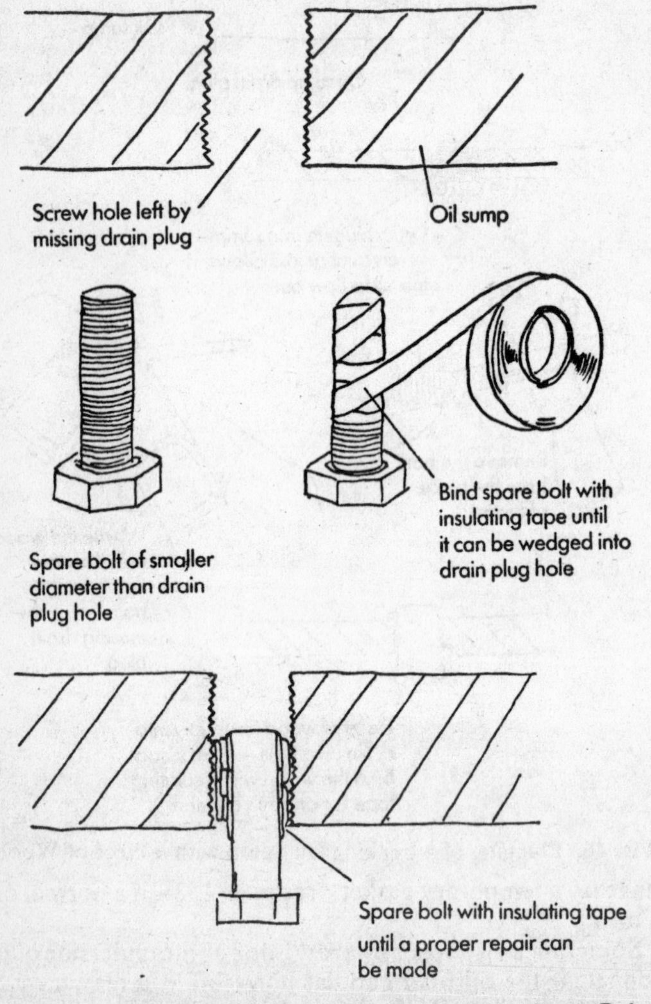

Fig. 47: Plugging of a Leaking Oil Sump with a Spare Bolt

in fig. 46, so long as there are no loose pieces which might fall down into the hole.

3. *Before driving on, the oil level must be replenished to the full mark.*

If you have not been able to establish a reason for the loss of oil it will probably become obvious within a 100 metres or even within a few seconds of trying to start the engine, if the leak is serious. So keep looking, till satisfied there is no massive leak. If you have "cured" any leak on the lines described above, you must check your handiwork frequently, and you must watch for the warning light, until you can have a proper repair made as soon as possible.

DO NOT OVER-FILL THE OIL.

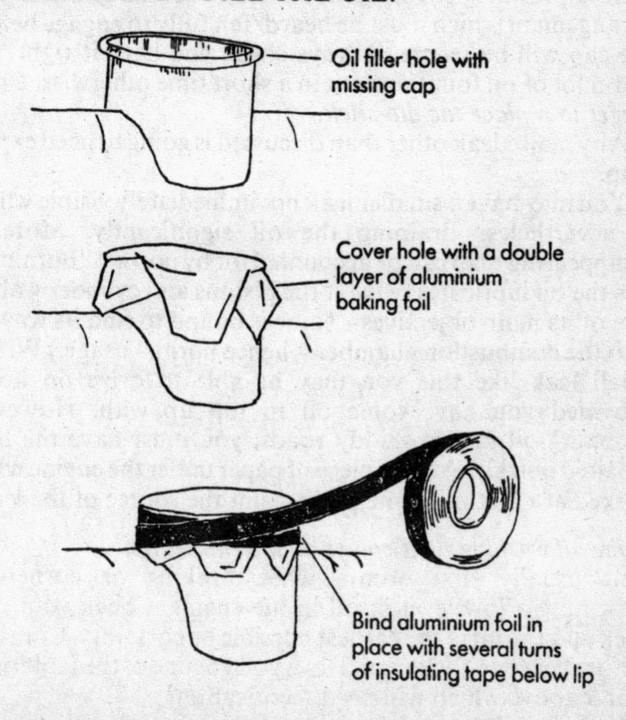

Fig. 48: Temporary Replacement of an Oil Filler Cap
There is considerable lifting pressure on a cap when the engine is running. especially at high speeds. Never rely on your handiwork without frequent checks to be sure it stays on.

Over-filling with oil can cause undue pressure in the system and lead to all sorts of problems which are very expensive, e.g. cylinderhead gasket blown, etc.

Find out from the owner's instruction handbook how much oil is required to raise the level from MIN to MAX. Always put in less than this guidance suggests, wait a minute for it to find its way sumpwards and check the dip-stick (as described in fig. 14 page 32) to see how much more you may need.

MAKE SURE YOUR OIL-FILLER CAP "CLICKS", LOCKED ON.

Most types turn clockwise to do up. No more than half a turn is probably involved but there is normally a slot/key arrangement which must be heard/felt fully to engage before the cap will be secure. Always check you have it right. An awful lot of oil fountains out in a short time otherwise. *Don't forget to replace the dip-stick.*

Any major leak other than discussed is going to need expert help.

You may have a smaller leak not immediately visible which is nevertheless draining the oil significantly. More is disappearing than can be accounted for by normal "burning". (As the oil lubricates betwixt the pistons and cylinder walls – one of its main objectives – some is bound to find its way up into the combustion chamber – hence normal usage.) With a small leak like this you may be able to drive on home provided you have some oil to top up with. However, dropping oil makes skiddy roads; you must have the leak repaired quickly. A large piece of paper under the engine while parked at night might help pin-point the source of the leak.

If the oil warning light comes on intermittently:
This usually first occurs when braking or cornering, indicating a low level of oil in the engine. Check your dip-stick and top up at the earliest possible opportunity. Consider *why* it started to flicker on. Have you got one of the faults in 1, 2 or 3 above which will need rectification?

You may have a faltering switch or wiring which only short-circuits intermittently, depending on bumps in the road or sharp bends etc. See pages 65 and 121. However, that would be an unusual cause to encounter.

8B *Charging light comes on*
This indicates a failure of the charging system which means that the car will be drawing all its electrical energy from the battery, rather than the alternator/dynamo. In older cars with dynamos the light may flicker on and off at engine idling speed but it should go out and stay out as soon as the accelerator is touched, however lightly. If it tends to stay on brightly at anything above idling speed without any flicker, you may not be in trouble now (unless it doesn't go out at all) but a charging system overhaul is worth putting in hand. You may need new dynamo brushes (an expert job), for example. With an alternator the light should go out directly the engine runs and stay out. To identify whether you have an alternator or dynamo see Chapter 4, page 31, fig. 12 and fig. 49.

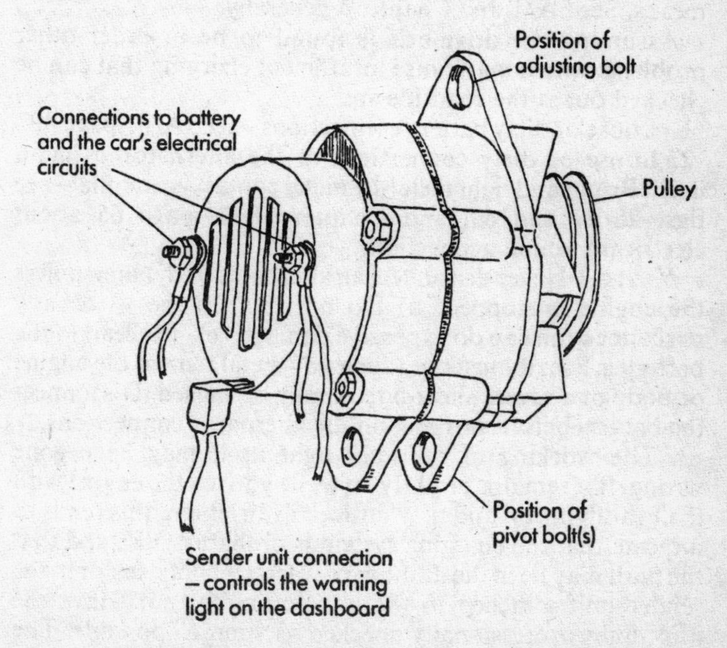

Fig. 49: Electrical Connections to the Alternator
The connections to a dynamo are similar in appearance. The connections vary in design depending on make, model and age of car, and can either be screw-type (as illustrated), spade terminals or push-on "block" terminals.

A charging light which comes on while you are driving needs immediate investigation.

Most commonly it will mean trouble at the drive-belt; the belt may be loose or may even have snapped. If that is the case and you do nothing, you will soon have overheating and all the trouble that goes with that – not to mention the risk of major expense. See Chapter 7C/2 and 7C/3. Some engines have a separate water pump drive belt, and an electrically driven fan. On these types the car can still be driven a short way to get help even though the alternator drive has failed. How far you can get will depend how quickly the battery wears down but you are saved the possibility of overheating. If the fault is elsewhere in the charging system and you ignore it, you will soon have a flat battery with all the aggro that means. See 5A/1 and Chapter 5 generally.

Assuming the drive-belt is found to be in order other problems which may cause insufficient charging that can be checked out at the roadside are:

1. Loose or dirty battery connections – see 5A/6, page 49.

2. Loose or dirty connections at the alternator/dynamo itself. Bright and tight metal-to-metal contact is essential – see figs. 26/27 and 49, and Chapter 5B/3, page 65 about electrically sound connections.

Note: a) Never disconnect an alternator or dynamo unless the engine is stopped. b) Do not mix up the wires; any misconnection can do expensive damage. c) The lead to the battery is live; it must not touch any metal part of the engine or body or a severe short-circuit may be caused. Disconnect the battery before working on the alternator connections.

3. The working of the idiot light itself may have gone wrong. If it remains brightly on while you rev the engine with the headlights on and they noticeably brighten, this tends to indicate that the charging system is probably O.K. and that the fault may lie in the dashboard warning light itself or in the sender unit attached to the alternator/dynamo. Have the idiot light professionally checked as soon as possible. The charging rate can then also be monitored to see if it is up to scratch.

However, if the light "blinks" unsteadily at higher revs instead of going out, you almost certainly have a major alternator/dynamo or charging fault beyond our scope.

Hopefully you will have enough juice left in the battery to drive to an electrical repair specialist – using as few electrics as possible on the way there.

4. You may have noticed failure of the charging light to come on at all. Try the headlight test in 3) above. If that shows some charging is happening, again you need the warning light itself put right, and it's probably worth having the charging rate tested.

8C *Temperature warning light comes on or gauge hits "Danger" or red sector*

Stop!

Switch off the engine. Turn to the overheating Chapter, 7.

9
ENGINE MISFIRES

Loss of power through misfiring can quickly worsen to the point when something must be done if you are to get home safely. Sometimes over-heating results too, see chapter 7 if need.

Nearly always, misfiring can be traced to worn sparking plug(s) or contact breaker points, just as we find when the Engine Won't Go. See Table 1, page 41. A new set of each may save you a lot of investigative time. If these are nearing replacement (10 to 12,000 miles running) there is no loss in changing them; a cured misfire will be bonus! See 5B/4, 2, page 80, and 5B/3, page 68, 1) to 6). Otherwise start with a look at Table 7 which follows. Table 7 sends you directly to the section of the book which should then help.

9A *Finding The Missing Cylinder*
As you can receive a shock this test is not for the faint-hearted.

Start the engine. SAFETY: keep hands, ties etc. clear of moving parts. Have the engine ticking over and, using a pair of insulated pliers to avoid a sharp unpleasant shock, pull off one HT lead from its sparking plug. Wearing rubber or other gloves *as well* can help insulate you from shocks.

If that plug has been working properly there will be an immediate drop in engine performance. If that plug was *not* sparking there will be *no* difference. Stop the engine.

If the plug is proved out of order investigate that plug and/or its lead as suggested in Table 7. Otherwise restore its lead and carry on along the same procedure with the other plugs in turn. Always stop the engine before putting a plug lead back; this helps you avoid shocks. Note that it is always worth testing all the plugs, as more than one might not be sparking full time.

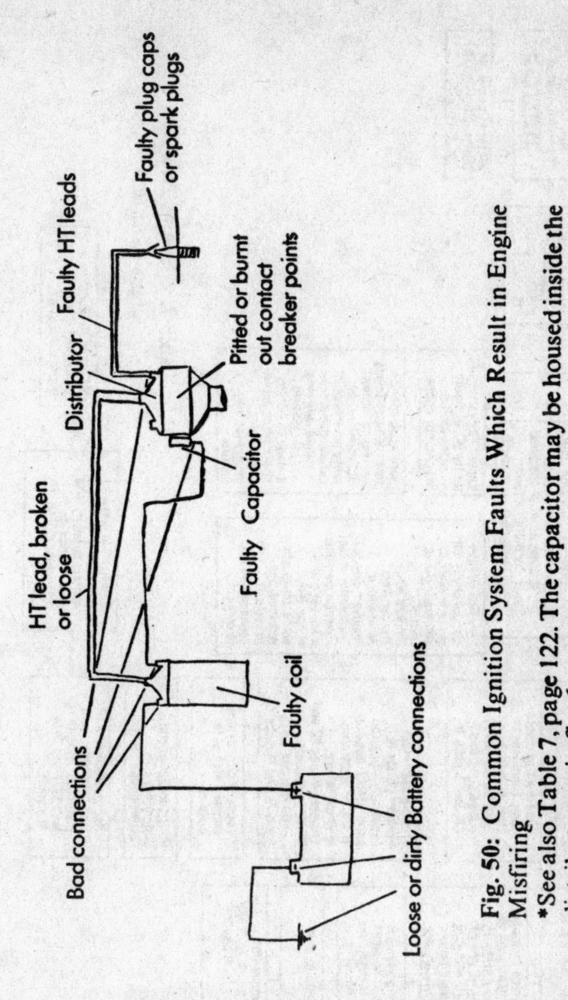

Fig. 50: Common Ignition System Faults Which Result in Engine Misfiring
*See also Table 7, page 122. The capacitor may be housed inside the distributor as in fig. 6.

9B *Ignition Wire Waggle Test*
Sometimes an LT or HT wire/lead is loose or even broken, or it has chafed on a sharp edge allowing an electrical short-circuit. Bumps in the road or whatever "make or break" at the trouble spot giving rise to an irregular misfire. If you work your way round all the get-at-able LT and HT wires/leads, using figs. 50, and 25 and section 5B/3 page 63, while the

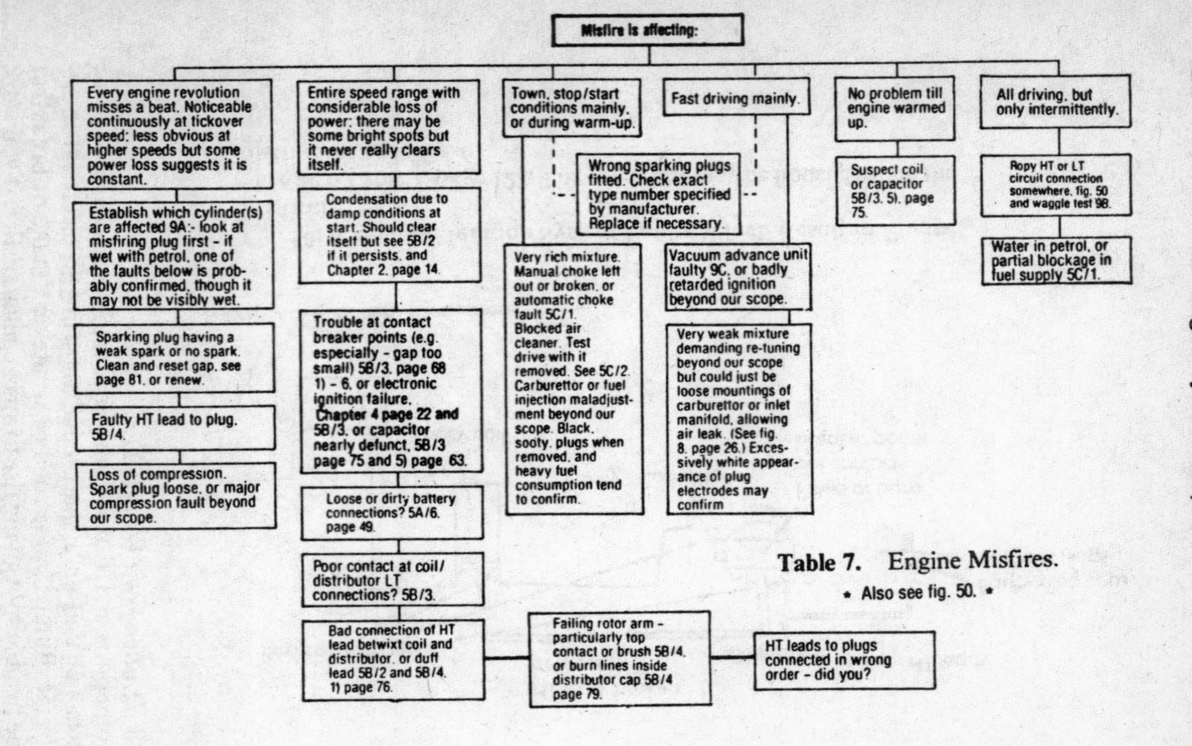

Table 7. Engine Misfires.

* Also see fig. 50. *

engine is running, you may well track down the fault. SAFETY: remind yourself of the dangers of a running engine – see page 11. Don't let the excitement of the hunt let you forget – even for a moment. As in the spark plug test (9A above) you can get an electrical shock; it is when you jump that you are liable to forget safety . . . Use rubber or other gloves *and* insulated pliers.

Waggle as if you meant it but not so hard as to cause a fresh break. Listen to the engine beat as you do so. When you hear your misfire disappear – OR, perhaps *re-appear* – you are on to the source of the misfire, in that wire/lead or its connections. To repair the fault refer to Damaged LT wires, page 65, High Tension Circuit check 5B/4 generally, and 1), page 79, Battery connections 5A/6, page 49.

9C *To Check Vacuum Advance Unit*

This device can be seen in fig. 3, page 21. It depends on the suction that is created as the fuel enters the engine and this suction varies according to load and accelerator position. The purpose of the unit is to advance the ignition at just the right times and always in the right relationship with power requirements. The spark is thus delivered to the plug earlier whenever the demands on the engine so require.

The only fault which you can do much about at the roadside is if something has gone wrong with the suction factor, i.e. if the pipe has become detached or if there is clearly a leak in it. Make sure that the pipe is firmly attached at the vacuum advance unit if there looks to be any doubt about that. This may solve the problem. If not, detach the pipe and run the engine with your finger over the end of the detached pipe. If an assistant can rev the engine up and down you should feel definite suction rising and falling in unison with the engine revs. If you cannot feel that, look for cracks or leaks along the pipe, or detachment or bad fitting of the pipe at its other end. Cracks could be taped up with insulating tape on a temporary basis. If the vacuum advance unit has failed internally, repair will be a garage job.

10

TOWING AND TOW STARTS

10A *Essential Things to Know*

If you want to try a tow start, read the beginning of Chapter 6 and section 6A for essential background information.

Both for a tow start and for distance towing the driver of the *towing* vehicle has a huge responsibility. The extra risk being taken gives rise to a grey area as regards both drivers, both in insurance terms and in law. Readers must decide for themselves whether they are taking on a task for which, should anything go wrong, they really are prepared to accept the consequences. For example, it would seem reasonable for the towing vehicle to display hazard warning flashers all the time (except for the signalling stage of turns) but the law provides that you must not have 4-way flashers on, on the move. (Personally, I would rather risk a fine . . .) If the towed vehicle has a completely flat battery and therefore has no horn, no brake lights etc., is it a safe vehicle under the Construction and Use Regulations Law of which extracts are reprinted in the back of the Highway Code, and so on? What does your insurance policy lay down on the matter?

The towing driver must maintain a constant mirror watch in case the back driver needs to stop. He must allow for the fact that the back vehicle may have no choice but to "cut" the corner as a turn is being made. Above all, *he must allow time when pulling across another lane* (e.g. crossing a major road – or turning right, off one) for the back car's safe passage – remembering the rope could snap just at the wrong moment! Starting and stopping must all be done in "slow motion" to avoid jerking the tow rope or catching the back driver unawares. Speed must be low (I strongly recommend 30 mph absolute maximum); anticipation in order to avoid sharp stops must be super-high.

The driver being towed has the main responsibility for keeping the rope taut so that it does not keep having slack taken up, with the jerk threatening to snap the rope. His reactions to the front driver's brake lights/arm signals need to be acute but without neglecting his general road reading/anticipation/driving safety. For a tow-start, it is important that the rope is taut before you let the clutch pedal up.

SAFETY

* Agree the STOP signal *before* you start. The "I intend to slow down or stop" arm signal in the Highway Code is the best *because other road users see it too.* (Headlight flashing or horn blowing can be reserved for desperation – *by agreement* – but note they do not work with a flat battery.)

* Power assisted steering or servo-brakes need heavy hands and foot when the engine is not running – to replace the power assistance!

* The ignition key/switch has to be *fully on* in order to free the steering lock and to provide brake lights and winkers, wipers, horn etc. See also 10B, 4.

* Your tow rope must be secure. See 10B. I suggest the *minimum* separation of the vehicles needs to be 4 metres.

* Display the words "ON TOW" prominently at the back of the towed vehicle. If possible, display the word "TOWING" on the front of the front vehicle. In daylight keep headlights on, full beam.

* Some cars, particularly automatics, for technical reasons cannot be towed without the driving wheels raised off the ground! Consult your owner's operating handbook. Some must not be towed backwards. A professional tow may be the only alternative.

* Manual transmission cars should be in neutral. With

automatic transmission the selector lever is normally required to be at "N" but you must consult your owner's operating handbook (see above).

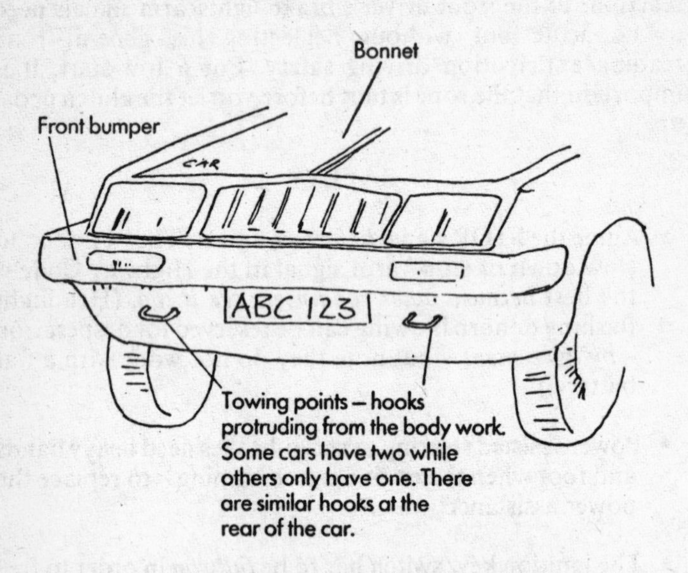

Fig. 51: Finding the Towing Points

10B *Detailed Tips*

1. The correct attachment point for the tow line should be found by referring to the owner's operating handbook for each car. You may have fitted towing eyes as depicted by fig. 51 or you may just have to find a *substantial* under-body cross member at your own risk. Do not tie near the exhaust pipe. It will melt or burn through rope! Keep the rope clear of moving parts which could get entangled and pipes which could get trapped, especially brake hydraulic pipes. Avoid sharp edges which will sever rope in a trice.

2. Nylon rope, which has more "give", and is of immensely greater breaking strain, is preferable to natural fibre rope. If you know a strong reliable knot, fine, use that for tying the rope. If not, you will find Julie's Hitch is excellent and marvellously adjustable. The knot comes from Geoffrey

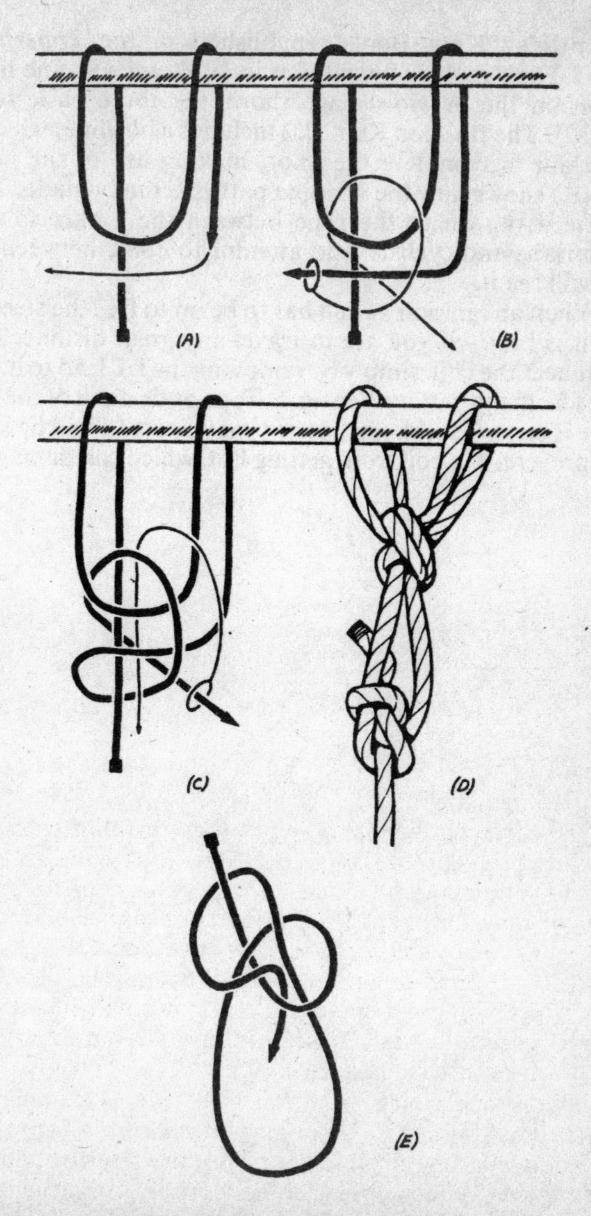

Julie's Hitch – for tow-rope attachment

Budworth's "Knot Book" (published in the *Paperfront* series). His daughter invented it in 1974, aged 9! The illustration on the previous page shows the three basic steps (A)–(C). The finished Knot (D) includes a bowline, which is important to complete the knot, making use of the loose end. (E) shows how the bowline part is actually made.

3. Tie a rag on to the rope between the 2 cars so that pedestrians and cyclists who attempt to come between the two, will see it.

4. When an ignition switch has to be on to free the steering lock it is best – if you are to travel any great distance – to disconnect the coil, simply by removing the LT lead to it that comes from the battery. See fig. 5. Tape or tie it out of the way where it cannot spark against any metal part (it will be live). This prevents the coil from getting hot, which can damage it.

11

SHATTERED WINDSCREEN

Laminated windscreens may crack but do not usually shatter or craze-over. However glass is heavy and a serious crack needs equally serious thought as to whether it could blow in at speed, with consequent danger to driver/passengers.

Toughened glass screens craze-over in an all too familiar way. The crazing usually takes several seconds, during which time you can pull up safely (after consulting your rear-view mirror), provided you concentrate your eyes on the road and not the splintering glass. Never wait till the crazing-over is complete. Safe vision is decimated at the outset.

The best remedy is an emergency windscreen as recommended in Chapter 2, which simply stretches across and is mainly held in place by being jammed in the doors. They come with full instructions.

In the absence of such an emergency screen, I personally recommend calling a radio-controlled emergency replacement service rather than making a hole in the crazed screen and trying to drive on. There are just too many tiny slivers of glass (almost too small to see) to be blown about, perhaps into an eye, not to mention the risk of stones etc. thrown up by traffic ahead. However, if you must drive, then:

1. Before trying to remove the glass, stuff heater vent slits etc., with handkerchiefs, rags, etc., to prevent glass falling into heater system.
2. Punch a good-sized hole in the crazed-over windscreen, wearing either a glove or with a piece of cloth wrapped around your hand, or tap it gently with a spanner. Take the hole right up to the top, at least in the area you will need to see through for driving, so that no more glass is likely to fall out into your face.
3. Wear glasses, or sun-glasses (only in daylight . . .) if you have them, in order to try and protect your eyes.

4. Drive slowly. Your insurance and/or a Court will take a very dim view of any accident.
5. Do not drive more than a few miles and certainly no further than absolutely necessary.

12

BROKEN WINDSCREEN WIPERS AND WASHERS

By Law "... windscreen wipers and washers ... should be maintained in effective working order at all times." Since you are also under a legal obligation to keep windows and windscreen clean and clear (something few drivers appear to appreciate!), if your wipers fail in rain you are stuck, both practically and legally! Fortunately, because there is little that can be done about it at the roadside, wiper motors are very reliable and rarely grind to a halt. Occasionally the motor works but doesn't move the wiper(s); the nut which secures the bottom of the wiper arm to the splined motor spindle simply needs tightening.

12A *Failed Windscreen Wipers*
The first check is to see if the fuse that controls the wipers has burned out. If other electrical items have stopped too, there is a good chance the fuse has blown. Chapter 4, page 34 helps you locate the fuse-box. Hopefully you are carrying spare fuses as recommended in Chapter 2. A code to tell you which is the fuse concerned should be found in the owner's operating handbook, or may be printed inside the fuse-box lid or somewhere nearby. Without the code you need to inspect all the fuses in turn ... They simply pull out. From its appearance it will be obvious if a fuse is blown. Although fuses differ in design they all consist of a thin wire, stretched across either a porcelain insulator (see fig. 52), or between metal ends inside a glass tube. As in a household fuse, if the wire has burned through, the fuse is blown.

A blown fuse must be replaced. There are *no* safe alternatives.

If a fuse has blown you want if possible, to avoid blowing your spare fuse immediately! Sometimes a fuse blows for no other reason than that it is tired and old. The new fuse solves the problem. More often, there is a circuit fault and the fuse blew to protect the wiring from a burn-out.

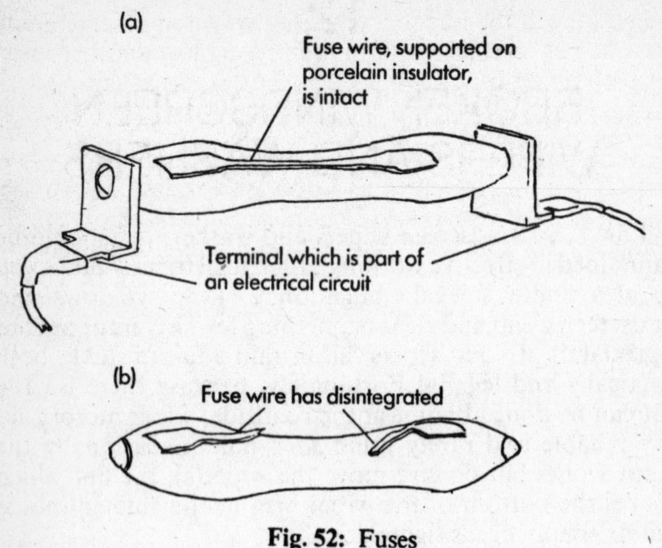

Fig. 52: Fuses
(a) Functional, and
(b) Blown

Having replaced the fuse *with one of the same rating*, inspect, clean and tighten the wiper motor electrical connections if they are accessible, *before* trying the wipers. Look for the wiper motor under the bonnet (see page 17 if you need to know how to open the bonnet). It has to attach to the bottom of one of the wiper arms or to a connecting link between two arms. It is usually about the size of a large grapefruit; a connecting link is often contained in a tube and therefore no moving parts are visible. Have the ignition turned *off*. Fingers can be trapped when a motor suddenly goes – and it is *very* powerful!

If the fault was in the electrical connection, with any luck you may clear it and not blow another fuse in the car, or in your head! If the fuse does blow at once when you do switch on the wipers you need expert help.

If the wipers now work but you have no more spare fuses (maybe you even borrowed an equivalent one from an unimportant circuit . . .), resist the temptation to switch on anything else unessential controlled by that fuse (e.g. rear window wiper) until you have access to some more spare fuses. You will then be in a position to switch on each item controlled by that fuse in turn, until you blow another fuse, thus identifying the circuit which needs expert attention.

12B *Failed Windscreen Washers*
Open the bonnet (page 17 if need) and find the washer bottle. Track the tubes from the outlet nozzles back to the bottle, if you are not sure which bottle it is. If it is empty, undo the top and fill it up with water that contains either a screen-wash additive or a few drops of washing-up liquid. In winter the proper additive containing anti-freeze is essential, or you will find the washers' tubes/nozzles can even freeze up as you drive along. On a motorway remember, a sudden loss of washer ability can be a major hazard. In arctic weather it is essential to run the windscreen demister at full heat *prior* to operating the washers; otherwise the washer fluid will freeze as it hits the glass – and your wipers will spread an instant film of ice across your vision.

If the bottle cap has a tube leading out of it as some do, make sure that when the cap is back on, the tube is pushed in so as to reach down inside to the bottom of the bottle – from whence it needs to suck.

If emptiness was not the problem, you need to check the motor and the pipework. If someone else can operate the washer switch while you listen at the motor, you will hear it humming immediately if it is working. If it is not working, inspect, clean and tighten the electrical connections and/or look for a blown fuse just as explained above in 12A. If the motor still will not work you will need a replacement. You may be interested to know that motorists' D.I.Y. stores and motor factors sell new motors considerably cheaper than the car maker's brand-name spare parts. If you are any good at all at small-scale "engineering" you can fit such a motor and save yourself quite a lot of money.

If the motor does hum and the bottle is full it may take a few seconds for the screen-wash fluid to reach the outlet nozzle. Since the pipework is normally transparent, if you follow it out you may well see where there is a blockage or a kink which is causing the problem, and which will be a relatively simple matter to straighten out or clear. A blockage might be on the inlet side of the pump, i.e. inside a dirt-ridden bottle. If the end of a pipe has become detached anywhere you may need to cut a small piece off before re-attaching it in order to get a good airtight fit. If the fault has yet to be discovered, have a little tug at each connection in order to make sure that air getting in is not the source of your problem; treat any suspect connection as above. A drop of saliva or soap helps the pipe push fully onto the stub.

The nozzles themselves can become blocked and a pin is the right tool to clean them out. It is as a rule, also *the* specialist tool required for redirecting the nozzles onto the screen if the washer fluid is not spraying on to just the right place. Stick the pin into the hole in the nozzle and use it as a lever to redirect its fire. Trial and error soon finds the best position.

13

LIGHT FAILURE

The Law is strict about lights and you should be aware that the police do enforce it. Both brakelights, and all winkers must always work (although arm signals may theoretically suffice, I would not care to test the matter in court even if I could prove my journey had been solely to buy a new bulb). At night you must have all 4 sidelights and both headlamps working as well. Hence I recommend carrying spare bulbs in Chapter 2, page 16. The latest cars have a dashboard "idiot" light to tell you of a failed lamp. Good drivers, by habit, surreptitiously observe their lights at opportune moments in shop windows etc., or have a regular routine all-round test with an assistant.

13A *Blown Fuse*

If several bulbs are out, or more than one electrical system is affected, for example rear screen demister/wash-wipe and brakelights, check the fuse as described in Chapter 12A. As suggested there, if it has blown and you only have one spare fuse (which MUST be of the correct rating) check the electrical connections (to all the units concerned) before switching anything on. Only switch on the item(s) of necessity until you have some more fuses and can afford to risk another. You may be lucky in finding the offending component is one you do not need, and that you are thus enabled to drive on. If unlucky and the fuse blows again straightaway you need an expert to rectify the basic fault. If the fuse does not blow again when you do come to try all the units at once, the new fuse may have been all you needed but it is nice to be safely at home before you chance making sure! (If the fuse is O.K., the trouble may be at the main battery terminals – see 5A/6, page 49 – but this is only likely if more than just one or two electrical systems are affected.)

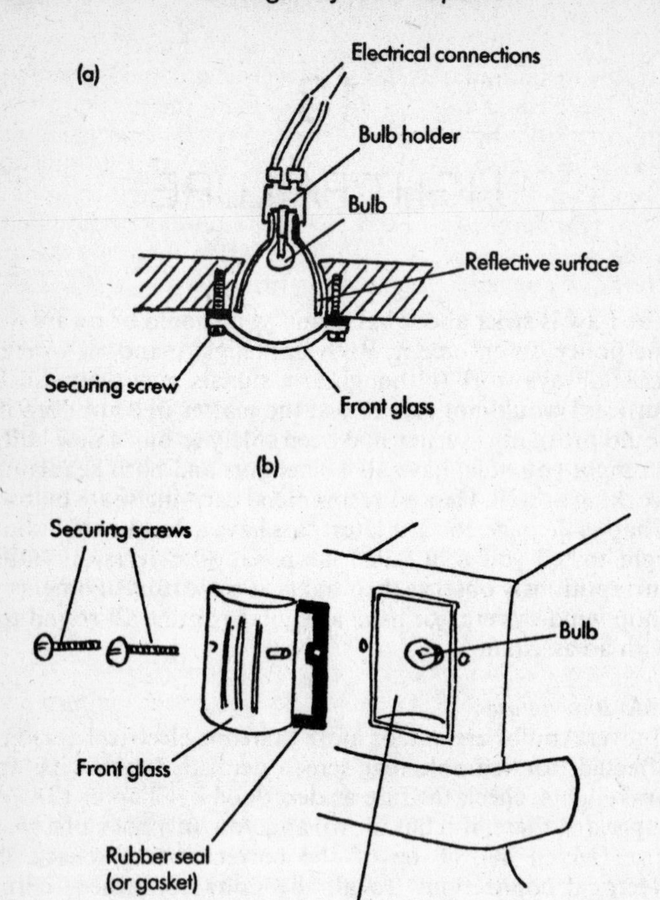

Fig. 53: Replacement of a Sidelight Bulb
(a) Cross section of a Sidelight
(b) Replacement

13B *Individual Lamps Out*
The most likely cause is bulb failure or, for sealed headlamps, of that unit. A replacement is needed and how to fit it is always explained in the owner's operating handbook. In the absence of the handbook careful scrutiny of the lamp

assembly inside and outside should reveal an obvious way in which the bulb can be got at. Look from the inside of the bodywork first, perhaps behind a removable trim panel; if there is no access via the inside, the way to the bulb is probably via unscrewing the outer glass as described in fig. 53. For rear lamps, a whole cluster of bulbs may be mounted on one pop-out panel reached from inside the body. Most bulbs have a bayonet type two-pin fitting just as in the U.K. domestic light-bulb. Push, twist anti-clockwise and release, and out it comes. The pins are usually off-set, so the bulb only fits one way round.

If on inspection the bulb looks sound (although looks are not everything!), or it works when transferred to the equivalent paired lamp on the other side of the car, or a new bulb is found *not* to work, the next most likely problem is a faulty earth.

Note: Keep bulbs squeaky clean; the grease of a thumb print can tarnish the reflector (fig. 53), via migration when the bulb heats up.

13C *Faulty Earths and Bad Connections*

If a bulb has been acting "dicky" without going out completely, or a good thump with the back of the hand on the bodywork near the lamp brings it on, a faulty earth is chief suspect. Chapter 4, page 34 explained how the earth return is usually made via the body of the car. The headlamps are normally an exception to this, having an independent earth return wire but all other lamps earth via the body, initially through the socket and the reflector.

When a headlamp fails, the thing to do is undo the connector which brings the wires to the back of it (normally a multiple push-on type), clean up the exposed metal surfaces and make sure it pushes back on with a tight and bright metal-to-metal fit (see fig. 26, page 66). For a failed headlamp, that is about all you can do at the roadside, unless it is of a type with a separate bulb and you have a spare bulb to try.

For all other lamps – once you have checked that the input connection is sound beyond suspicion as above – suspect the earthing. Remove the bulb and attend to the inside of the socket. Scrape rust and verdigris away completely. Re-fit the bulb. If it is rather loose, waggle it with the switch on. If it then works, you may be able to fashion some silver cigarette paper or aluminium baking foil to wrap round the side earthing contact on the metal body of the bulb, in such a way that it will fit back more tightly and make a satisfactory earth connection.

If nothing has worked so far and you know you are dealing with a sound bulb, there may be a break in the input wire which would be hard to find, or the way in which the reflector itself carries the current to earth into the bodywork may be at fault. Sometimes there is a small wire joining the outside of the reflector to a major body structure in which case the connections should be taken apart, cleaned and replaced, and sometimes the earthing continuity depends on the reflector being located soundly into the bodywork of the car. If you can get the reflector out and clean everything up you may solve the problem. If you have some household flex as recommended in Chapter 2, you can bypass the body earth by connecting the reflector direct to the battery earth, or some other good earth point nearby the light itself. Should that bring on the light you have proof it's an earth fault. If you can clear it you might be able to drive on with the temporary earth connection fastened in place.

The above things are the main roadside remedies. Any other problems remaining will be in the realm of electricians.

13D *Trouble With Winkers*

Failure of a single winker or, more usually, of front and back winkers on one side, should be investigated in the same way (for both lamps, because the fault may be due to failure of either one or both of them) as for other individual lamps in 13B and 13C. Replacement bulbs must be the right ones or the winkers will then flash too fast or too slow, probably outside the permitted frequency range.

When *none* of the four winkers work, first look at the appropriate fuse; see above, and Chapter 12A. Then check the terminals on the flasher "brain" unit, which must all be clean, tight and with good metal-to-metal contact (see fig. 26, page 66). The flasher unit should give an audible tick in time with the winking lights (partly to remind the driver it is on);

this may help you locate it – or it is down to detective work tracing the wires. Quite often the unit is under the dashboard. It consists of a metal case usually no bigger than half a Mars bar with at least three wires connected to it. One is the input, one goes to the panel repeater light, and one to the lamps themselves – via the indicator stalk switch which directs the current to the side required.

On older cars another similar but separate unit – usually mounted close by – is used to operate the hazard warning lights and therefore it is possible that although none of the winkers work when you try to indicate, the four-way flashers will still work. (If they do, you can rule out a fault at any of the bulbs.) On newer cars the two units may be combined into one item and there will be rather more wires emanating from it. These units either work by means of a solenoid inside, or in the latest cars the gadget is entirely electronic.

Whether you discovered one combined unit, or two separate units, attend as described to all the connecting wires individually in turn, so that there can be no mistake in fitting the right connection back on the correct stub.

Once you have done this, if the winkers still don't work you almost certainly need a new flasher unit. If they work but only on one side the problem is probably in the indicator stalk switch but is likely to be beyond roadside amateur repair.

If the winkers *come on* but don't flash, you need a new flasher unit. However, you may be able to "engineer" the necessary flashing by working the stalk arm switch appropriately, in order to get to a garage.

Apart from the latest electronic units, most flasher "brains" are worked by a magnetically-activated solenoid. This can sometimes jam. A gently repeated tap with a light screwdriver sometimes frees the solenoid allowing it to work again for the time being. As the unit is clearly unreliable it will have to be replaced as soon as possible.

If the dashboard panel "repeater" light fails, check all flashers for proper working as above. It may just be the repeater bulb that needs replacement but never assume that, without checking.

13E *Brakelight Failure*
When one side only, fails, check the bulb and/or the earthing as in 13B and C above. If both fail, the trouble could be at the brakelight switch. This is located in the hydraulic pipeline, normally before that divides in order to transmit pressure to all four wheels. This book does not attempt to deal with brake failure itself which would always require expert help but if you are clever at finding your way round the car and in tracing the brake pipes back to the master cylinder, it should be easy to find this small unit to which electric wires are attached. The attachment of these wires may be all that is wrong. Try cleaning them up properly just as with other connections for which see above. If the brakelights now work you have probably solved the problem but if they do not, the switch is almost certainly faulty – unless both brakelight bulbs have failed simultaneously (which would be unlucky) or the relevant fuse has blown. Do not interfere with the switch itself, or the brake pipeline, unless you have the necessary expertise.

14

HEATER/DEMISTER FAILURE

Although this is a fringe subject for an emergency book, being cold is uncomfortable and can certainly affect your driving, and inefficient demisting can be lethal.

A badly heated car can be the first sign of coolant loss. Before you have an overheating emergency check the coolant level; see Chapter 7A. If that is the problem, full heating should be restored once it is filled up.

Not many roadside remedies are available. If the heater works but not the blower fan, check the fuse as in Chapter 12A, page 131 and/or Check and clean up the wiring connections to the blower (see fig. 27 and page 65). Your owner's handbook may assist you in discovering where the wiring connects.

When the blower fails you can at least maximise the heat reaching the screen by shutting all secondary vents and setting the heat direction control to "screen only". Refer to your owner's handbook. This may be your only hope of preventing the windscreen icing up, apart from a de-icer spray.

If the heater controls are mechanically connected to the heater, you may be able to observe behind the dashboard a joint/hinge that has come adrift, and to re-set the control from underneath, or string the joint together etc., for the time being.

Poor heating, together with an engine that takes a long time to warm up indicates a faulty thermostat. See Chapter 7E, page 103.

15

BURST TYRE – PUNCTURE

A bang, lumpy or bumpy steering, or when braking may be your first clue there is trouble, or you may be lucky to be forewarned by another motorist or pedestrian gesticulating in your direction . . . When returning to a parked car, the experienced driver habitually glances at all the wheels and will usually spot a soft tyre before it becomes a problem. Do not imagine that a slightly soft rear tyre is insignificant. It can have just as dramatic an effect on your steering and brakes as a soft front tyre.

With a burst or flat tyre, or one that is obviously well on the way down *never try to drive to a garage* even if it is only a short distance. Apart from the danger (and your legal position knowingly ignoring it) you will further damage the tyre and quite possibly the wheel hub. A perfectly repairable punctured tyre can be ruined in a few yards, and they are not cheap.

A burst tyre is not repairable. It can only be replaced; so the spare must be fitted. Punctures must be properly repaired by a tyre specialist who will vulcanise (heat treat) the repair, so, again, you need to fit the spare. However, read on.

15A *Slow puncture*

If you are in a position to pump the tyre up (see fig. 54) and it will stay up long enough, you could choose to go straight to a tyre specialist who can fit the spare for you and repair the puncture. You need to know just how fast your slow puncture is in order to judge if the tyre will remain pumped up safely until you get there; only the slowest punctures really allow for this course of action. To fit the spare tyre yourself refer to 15B. The problem may be a leaking valve. A finger moistened with spittle and brushed across the top of the valve (fig. 54) will leave a bubble there long enough to see if it blows up due

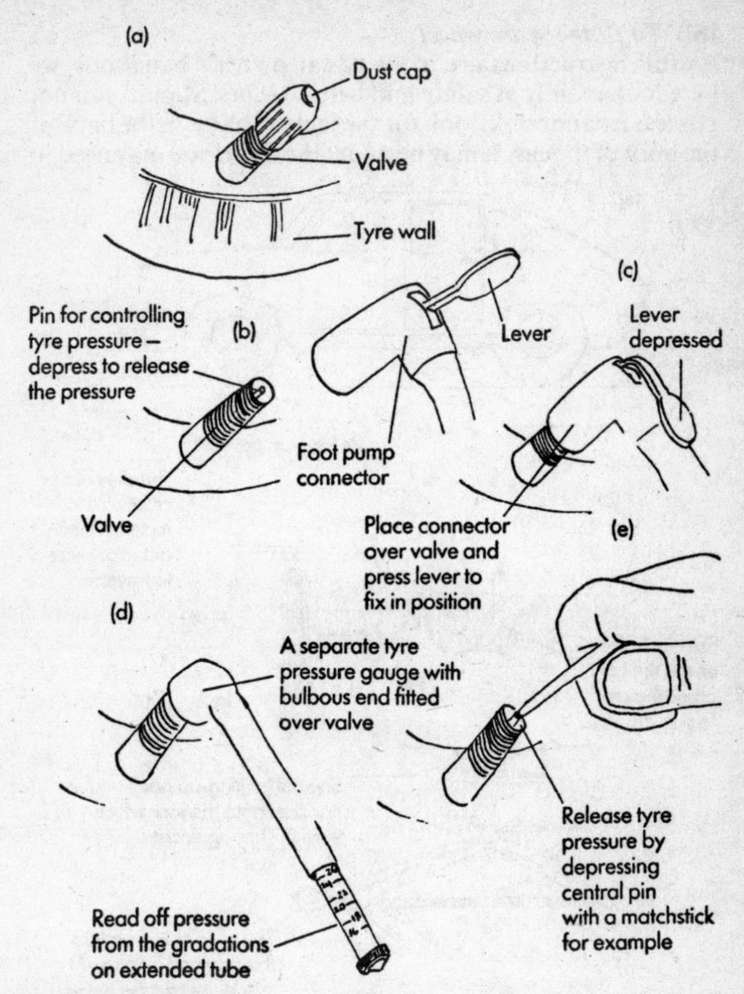

Fig. 54: Adjusting the Tyre Pressure if you have a Foot Pump and a Gauge
There must be no hiss of air loss when the gauge or pump connector are in place – a matter of trial and error in fixing it on firmly and squarely.

to any air leakage. A new valve can be fitted by a tyre agent without removing the wheel.

15B *To fit the spare wheel*
As full instructions are in every car owner's handbook we here look mainly at safety and helpful hints. Should you not possess a handbook, look for the jack/tool-kit in the back or the boot of the car. It may be under the floor; you may need to

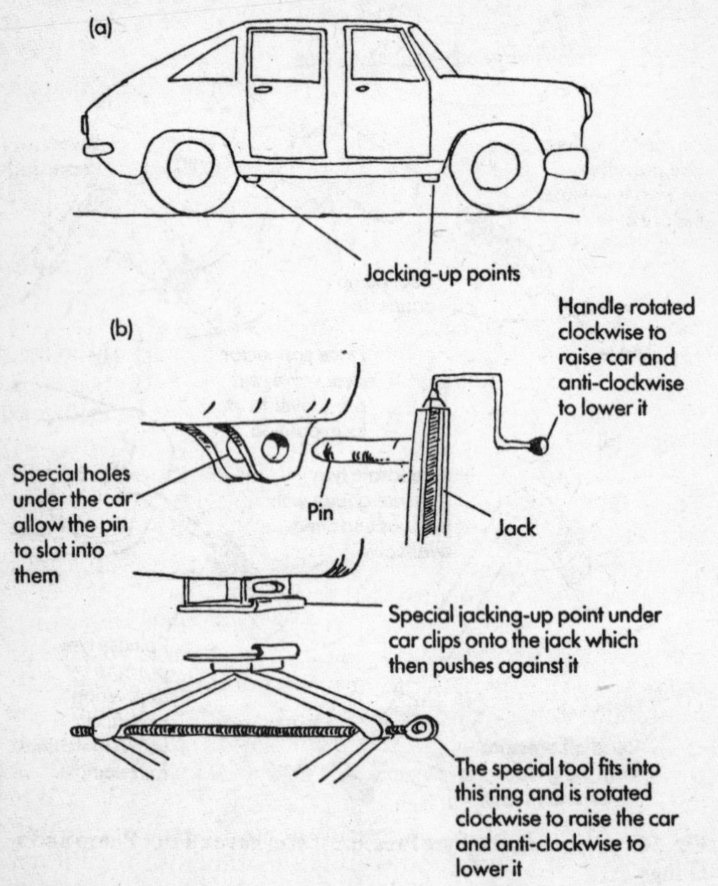

Fig. 55: The Jack and Jacking-Up Points
(a) Typical Locations of the Jacking-Up Points
(b) Different Types of Common Jacks. Pin, on "pillar" type, must slot fully home. Plate, on "scissors" type, must engage securely across its whole surface.

take out a removable trim panel. Sometimes the spare wheel is carried in an underbody tray and a winding down point – using one end of the wheel brace designed for that purpose – will be found under the rear carpet or below the boot carpet. Figs. 55, 56 and 57 and what follows below should help you work out the rest of the job.

SAFETY *and working order*:
The "Do's and Don'ts" on page 11 are vital. Please spare a few seconds to read them.

A few cars built when the law allowed it have a cheaper, space- saving spare wheel only intended for driving below a recommended speed for a minimal distance. Follow the instructions if you have one.

1. Make sure that the car is as far away from moving traffic as possible and that it is on flat ground. If on a hill you will have to manoeuvre under walking speed to get to a level place. Do not attempt the operation on any sort of incline. Note that your handbrake only works on the 2 front or the 2 back wheels, and that therefore the car will not be as firmly held as you might have imagined, once it is jacked up.
2. Switch off the engine. Pull on the handbrake firmly. Then, on an automatic transmission car, select "P" for park; with ordinary gears engage first or reverse. Chock the wheels on the side of the car *not* to be lifted. Do this securely for both directions with bricks or boulders etc.
3. *Promise yourself now* that you will not stick your head, legs or arms under the car, or sit down on the ground close to the car once it is held on the jack. Put yourself on red alert to jump back quickly should something happen. *Do not even consider* placing your explicit trust in the idea that the car will remain held safely by the jack – AT ANY STAGE OF THIS OPERATION.
4. When you place the jack ready in position make sure that the base of the jack is on level ground and not on uneven ground or on the edge of a hole (no matter how small). On soft ground place a solid piece of wood or similar item. under the jack so as to spread the load safely. Remember the jack must be fitted into the car's specific jacking-up point(s) described in your owner's hand-book. *Other places must not be tried.* Look at fig. 55 which illustrates common jacking-up

points and types of jacks and emphasises the care needed in fitting the jack properly to the jacking-up point.

5. Get the spare wheel out of the boot now, before starting to raise the car. Do not wait until later.

6. Remove any trim (fancy bits), and the shiny hub cap plate if fitted, from the wheel thus revealing the wheel nuts. If you cannot see how a hub cap comes off, lever it gently from the outside edge after getting a screwdriver blade behind it first. Most types "spring" off. Catch the hub cab before it rolls automatically – under sod's law – towards passing traffic.

7. Slacken off the 3, 4 or 5 wheel nuts you can now see by turning them anti-clockwise. Only slacken them. Do not

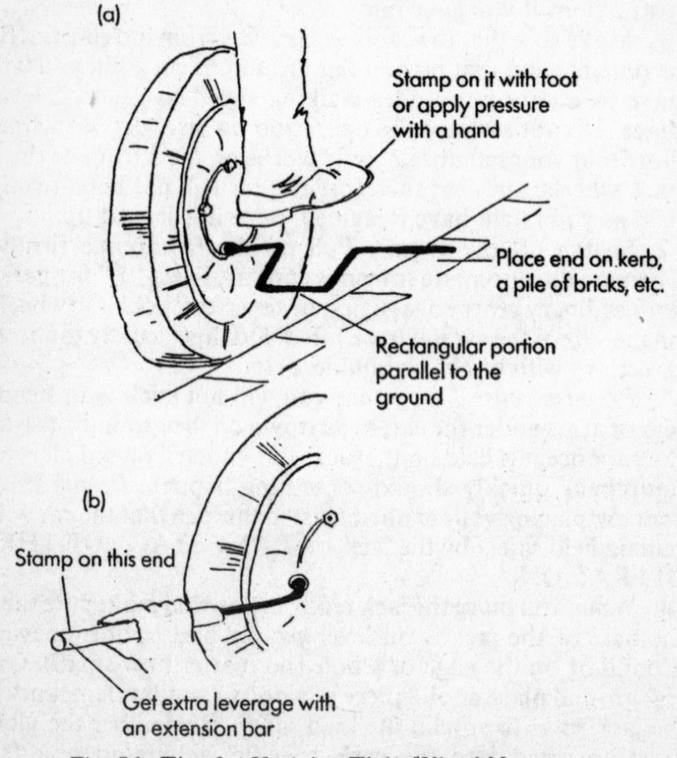

Fig. 56: Tips for Undoing Tight Wheel-Nuts
(a) With a "Rectangular" Wheelbrace Spanner
(b) With a "Right-Angled" Wheelbrace Spanner

undo them any more yet. The wheel-brace may double as the handle used to raise the jack, or it may be separate. Fig. 56 gives some tips if you find the nuts very tight. Be careful not to burr them. The wheel-brace or spanner must be kept firmly on the nut so that it cannot slip. Tight nuts are sometimes eased if tapped gently with a hammer a dozen times or so before you start.

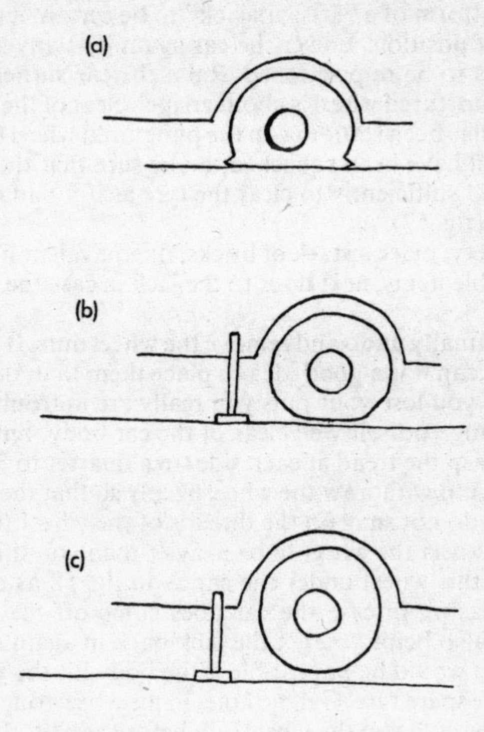

Fig. 57: The Correct Height for Jacking-Up the Car
(a) Punctured Tyre
(b) Incorrect Height. Although car may be jacked-up high enough to get punctured wheel off, there is insufficient height to replace with fully inflated tyre.
(c) Correct Height. The car is jacked-up high enough to allow the punctured tyre to come off and a fully inflated spare to go on.

8. Begin to raise the car up on the jack. From now on be *careful.* The car is unstable, being mainly supported on only 2 wheels and the jack. Watch while you continue and the car begins to lift, that the pin of a pillar jack remains securely right home. The top of the pillar usually inclines a little way away from the car to begin with. This is a deliberate safety feature so that when the car is fully raised the pillar will have moved in towards it and become exactly vertical. Keep an eye on the platform of a "scissors jack" to be certain it does not slip out of position. Lower the car again if at any stage the jack needs to be re-positioned. Raise the car sufficiently so that the punctured wheel is about an inch clear of the ground. If the car has been standing on the punctured wheel for some time it will have been squashed; make sure that the car has been raised sufficiently to clear the tyre as if it had not been squashed (fig. 57).

For safety, place a stack of bricks, or equivalent if you can find suitable items, next door to the jack in case the car does slip off it.

9. Now finally undo and remove the wheel nuts. If your car has a hub cap it is a good idea to place them in it, or in your pocket. If you lose your nuts you really are in trouble!

10. Keeping yourself well clear of the car body, remove the wheel. Clasp the tread at each side (in a quarter to 3 o'clock position) and withdraw the wheel evenly so that the holes in the wheel do not snag on the threads of the wheel studs (see fig. 58). Expect the wheel to be heavier than you think!

11. Slide this wheel under the car as in fig. 58 as a further safety measure in case the car does come off the jack (its presence also helps you get the jack back in again if it does fall, which would be impossible if the body hit the ground).

12. Fit the spare tyre. Get the holes in the wheel roughly lined up with the studs on the wheel hub before you lift the wheel.

13. Screw the wheel nuts back on clockwise, tightening them each a bit at a time in rotation, until they are all screwed fully home at least finger tight. The nuts normally have one end tapered, which is intended to fit snugly into the well-shaped edge of the hole in the wheel. It is vital not to screw them on the wrong way round.

14. Lower the car until the jack can be removed.

15. Then, again in rotation, a bit at a time, fully tighten the

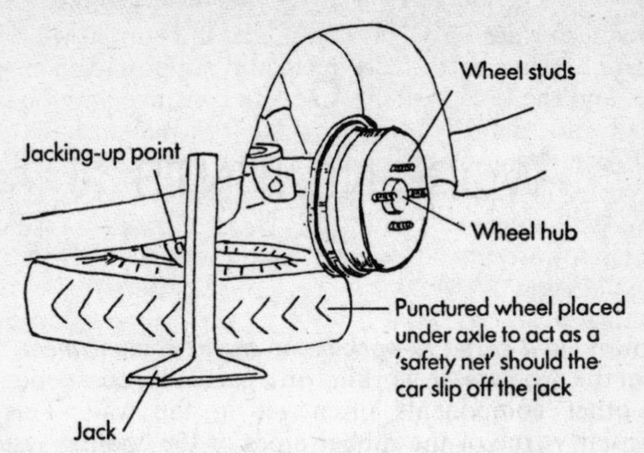

Fig. 58: The Use of the Punctured Tyre as a Safety Device by sliding it under a Jacked-Up Car.

wheel nuts. Make sure they are as tight as you are able to get them using the maximum leverage the car wheel-brace can provide on its own. (An extension bar could give you too much leverage.)

If you are not experienced about how tight they should be, have somebody who does know check them. Should you have to drive more than a mile or 2 – slowly! – to have this done, get out and check them yourself on the way.

16. Check and adjust the tyre pressure. See fig. 54 if you have the equipment, or drive slowly no farther than the nearest garage, to do it. (This assumes your spare tyre is not obviously flat!)

17. Remember to remove the chocks, flat-tyred wheel, jack etc . . .

18. Do not delay in getting a puncture fixed. Murphy's Law applies; if you delay you will get caught out with another puncture even if you have never had one before in your life!

16

WORKING HINTS

16A *Making it easier to work in the engine compartment*
One of the problems in working on a particular component is that other components often get in the way. This is particularly true of the rubber pipes of the cooling system which criss-cross the engine. Since it is impractical to remove them, tie a piece of string around them, pull them back out of the way (they are very flexible), and secure. Remember to remove the string and to put everything back once the job is finished.

16B *Slackening off tight nuts and bolts*
1. For tight nuts refer to Chapter 15B, 7), page 146.
2. It is always worthwhile tapping a tight nut gently before trying again.
3. Also effective, is to hold the spanner firmly to the nut and then give the spanner a sharp tap with the hammer on the end away from the nut. Prevent fingers at the nut end (from being jarred or pinched) by wearing gloves or using a piece of rag between your fingers and the spanner. Sometimes you can extend a spanner with metal tubing (see fig. 56).
4. Aerosol penetrating oil sprayed over a nut can magically allow what appeared an immovable nut to be undone after a few moments have elapsed for the oil to do its work. It is vital not to spray such oil anywhere near ignition electrics – where it would provide a leakage path for the electric current – because this could involve you in an awful lot of cleaning-up. Nor must you spray it, for example, near a disc-brake which could dangerously reduce the brake's efficiency.
5. The first 4 items above assume you have the correct size spanner, or a good adjustable spanner that is giving a tight fit. Without the proper equipment you run the risk of "rounding

off" between the flats of the nut, making it impossible thereafter to undo with a spanner.

If you have not got the right spanner there are 2 possible alternatives. One is if you have an adjustable self-grip "Mole" type wrench. The other is if you combine a loose-fitting spanner with a screwdriver blade inserted so that the spanner and blade wedge together in a decent fit. The risk with either of these methods is that the nut will be ruined in the process but you may decide that the chance of success makes the risk worthwhile.

16C *Undoing tight screws*

Most readers will be aware how essential it is for the screwdriver blade to fit the slot in the screw exactly, if a burred slot is to be avoided. Even then, with a very tight screw, a slot can easily be wrecked. One way which usually gets round this problem *providing you use it from the outset*, is to hold the blade of the screwdriver firmly down into the slot with all the pressure you can muster, while you use a pair of pliers at the bottom end of the blade next to the screw itself to do the turning. The method prevents slippage and places considerably more turning power at your fingertips.

16D *"An extra pair of hands"*

An adjustable self-grip wrench makes an extra pair of hands since it will grip on to anything without requiring you to hold it in position. For example, when trying to undo a nut and bolt you are often defeated because both ends turn at the same time. A second spanner or a pair of pliers can solve the problem, but keeping them in place may be easier said than done. A self-grip wrench in contrast, although it will turn to start with, soon jams against something thus enabling you to undo satisfactorily from the other end.

16E *Filter funnel*

For refilling or topping-up purposes a cheap funnel can be made by cutting in half an empty plastic lemonade bottle. With a piece of rag etc., you can even fashion a makeshift filter.

16F *Making a new gasket*
A temporary gasket to ensure a perfect seal between surfaces (e.g. see page 105) can be made from an ordinary piece of cardboard such as a breakfast cereal packet. The cardboard can be cut to the right shape by placing it on the component that requires it and rubbing gently; engine parts are always dirty and the outline including the various holes for securing bolts etc. will thus be imprinted on the cardboard, which can then be cut to the right shape.

16G *"Butter fingers"*
A pair of tweezers helps pick up screws, nuts etc. that are dropped (you will drop them no matter how careful you think you are!) in the inaccessible spots in the engine compartment. A magnet, perhaps attached to a piece of string, can be an extremely valuable companion.

If you cannot get a screw or a nut to stay in an awkward place long enough to allow you to get the thread to start to hold, a simple blob of grease, or even peanut butter, may help you out unexpectedly.

17

WARDING OFF EMERGENCIES

17A Routine checks
A simple maintenance routine carried out as a routine weekly, fortnightly, or monthly habit, depending how much driving you do, can mainly be carried out at your petrol filling station in a matter of minutes whilst you are there anyway. These are the items that really matter – including some which are of paramount importance to safety. None of them should be left for more than 1 month between checks even if you hardly use the car. These checks should also be made during extended journeys which use more than 2–3 tanks of petrol, i.e. more than a normal week's motoring. These routine checks are *not* intended to replace proper garage servicing which must also be carried out at the correct intervals.

Weekly/fortnightly/monthly checklist

Under the bonnet (to open, see Chapter 3)

Oil level	Page 112
Coolant level	Page 96
Screen wash bottle	Page 133
Brake fluid reservoir	See owner's handbook; if this needs topping up you need to know *why*. Seek expert advice at once. Let the expert attend to refilling

Clutch fluid reservoir	Ditto
Battery electrolyte level	17C below

Outside items

All lamps working	Page 135
Tyre pressures (remember the spare), and visual inspection	Page 143 and 17D below

17B *Checks every so many 1,000x miles*
As well as defusing trouble, these checks, which can be integrated with normal garage servicing intervals *during which some of them are done anyway*, can bring worthwhile running cost economies.

Each 5,000 miles

Sparking plugs	(Page 81) Clean and adjust electrodes gap (renew at 10 to 12,000 miles).
Contact breaker points	(Page 70) Ditto
Air filter	(Page 88) Turn paper element round; renew at 10,000 miles, or if badly congested with dirt.
Fan belt	(Page 101) Check tension; renew if rubber is beginning to perish or crack.
Automatic transmission oil	Check level, following directions in owner's instruction handbook.

Each 20,000 miles, or 2 years

Battery	(Page 49) If terminals are corroded, undo, clean up, smear with Vaseline and retighten.
Windscreen wiper blades	Well worth renewing at this time, despite the cost. They snap into position. Most Lego addicts will see in a trice how.
Brake fluid	This should be changed at least once every 2 years because it absorbs water over a period of time. Water acts differently under pressure compared with proper fluid.

17C *Battery electrolyte level*
If your battery is not a sealed maintenance-free battery, it will have either 6 (sometimes 12) round plastic caps along the top, or 1 or 2 elongated plastic caps as shown in fig. 59. Individual caps have to be unscrewed. The elongated type are removed in 1 piece but you may need a screwdriver or strong fingers to prise them off.

You can now look into each cell individually (from a respectable distance, see below) and check that what are called the battery plates, which you can see near to the top inside, are just covered by clear liquid. The liquid is the electrolyte and it should cover the plates completely but no more than that. You do not fill up the cell any further.

Do not touch the electrolyte. It is sulphuric acid based. Do not smoke as bubbles of inflammable gas rise out of the liquid all the time, even if you cannot see them. Keep your face clear,

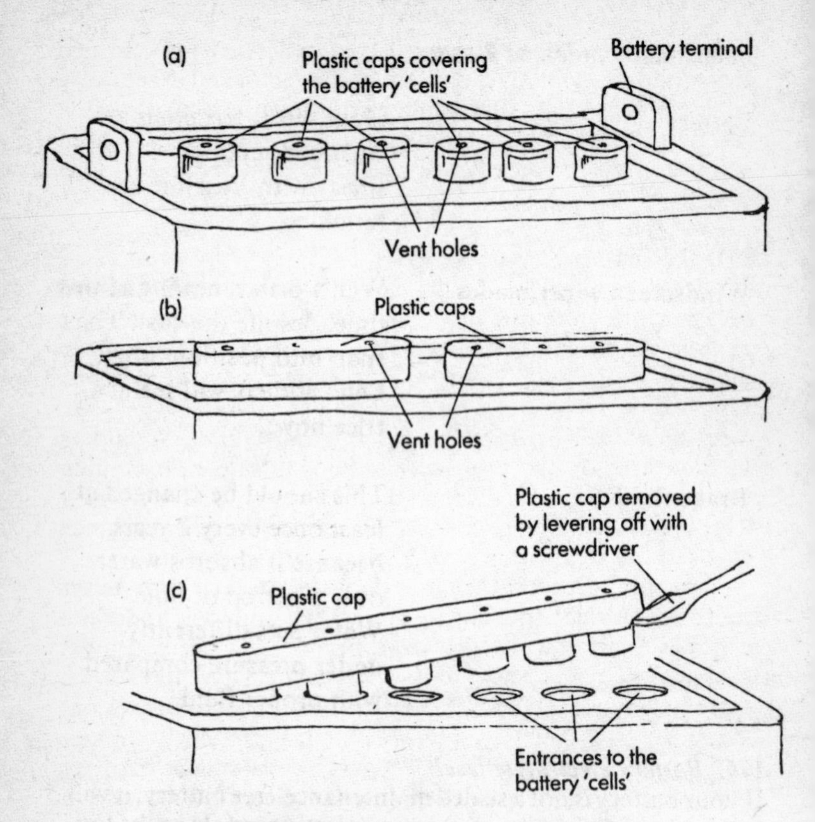

Fig. 59: Different Arrangements of Battery Caps
(a) Six Round Plastic Caps
(b) Two Elongated Plastic Caps
(c) One Elongated Plastic Cap

as little spits of acid due to the bubbling can harm the skin. Should you get any acid burn on your skin, wash immediately with copious amounts of water.

If the level of the electrolyte has fallen below the top of the plates bring it up to the right level by adding *distilled* water (sold at motorists' D.I.Y. stores, garages etc.). A possible substitute but one that must not be used every time because that would not be good for the battery, is rain water. Replace the plastic cap(s) having made sure that the vent holes in them are clear.

In practice a good battery will require virtually no distilled water and the vent holes will not become blocked except very occasionally. When that happens they can be cleared with a pin. Do not try to blow through them as they will have been splattered with acidic electrolyte and this can be painful to the lips.

17D *Visual inspection of tyres*

The regulations with regard to worn treads have changed several times in recent years. All tyre dealers display notices explaining the current rules, so that is the best place to keep yourself up-to-date as to whether your tyres need to be replaced.

Meanwhile, if you notice uneven wear, with the shoulders of the tread, or perhaps the middle of the tread, becoming worn much more quickly than the rest, you may save yourself a lot of money if you have the tracking and the wheel balance checked out straightaway by a garage or tyre agent.

You should examine *both* side walls of each tyre; never succumb to being too lazy to bend down and look under the car at the inside walls. Cuts and lumps are what you must look for. They are illegal. The walls of a car tyre have to be extremely flexible. Technology has made this possible but at the same time the walls have become progressively thinner and thinner. It is therefore a remarkably short time between the existence of a cut or a bulge being noticed and a potentially burst tyre. Hence the law. Hence the need for frequent examination by the driver. If you have bumped into the kerb, other than gently at parking speed (unless you do that daily!), examine the tyre(s) concerned straightaway and keep an eye on them to see that nothing untoward develops.

INDEX